365 TECHNICAL SERIES

I0062848

EFFECTIVE
IT TEAM
MANAGEMENT

LEADING AND EMPOWERING YOUR TECHNICAL TEAM

AMMAR AL ALOUSI

EFFECTIVE IT TEAM MANAGEMENT
FIRST EDITION

To my beloved wife, whose unwavering support and love make every journey worthwhile.

To my daughter and my two sons, who inspire me every day with their curiosity, strength, and dreams.

And to my father, Dr. Faiz Al Alousi, whom I lost too soon but who remains the guiding light in my journey. Your wisdom and legacy continue to shape my path, and I remain committed to carrying them forward.

Published in the United States of America
10 9 8 7 6 5 4 3 2 1

LIBRARY OF CONGRESS CATALOGING-IN-PUBLICATION DATA
LCCN: 2024927330

Names: Ammar Al Alousi, author.
Title: Effective IT Team Management: Leading and Empowering Your Technical Team / Ammar Al Alousi.
Description: Virginia: [2025] | Includes bibliographical references and index.

ISBN (Paperback): 979-8-9922795-0-4
ISBN (eBook): 979-8-9922795-1-1

Limit of Liability and Disclaimer

Trademark Disclaimer

FOREWORD

Managing an IT team today isn't just about keeping systems up and running or supervising skilled professionals. It's about leading a dynamic group through constant technological shifts, ever-changing business objectives, and evolving ways of working. I've been in the thick of it—facing these challenges head-on—and I've seen how strong leadership can turn tough situations into opportunities and help teams achieve remarkable things.

This book is for IT managers, whether you're stepping into leadership for the first time or you've been in the role for years. Inside, you'll find practical strategies, real-world examples, and adaptable tools to help you build, lead, and empower your team in today's fast-paced tech landscape. My hope is that these insights will inspire you to not just manage effectively but to lead with empathy, adaptability, and vision.

CONTENTS

| INTRODUCTION

The Importance of Effective IT Team Management

Being an IT manager is about more than just monitoring deadlines or assigning tasks. It's about creating a culture where technical know-how aligns with big-picture goals. It's about encouraging innovation, promoting accountability, and building teamwork. In our fast-moving industry, IT teams have to stay ahead of the curve, adopt new tools, adapt to changing demands, and find creative solutions to complex challenges.

As an IT manager, your role is to tap into your team's strengths, lead successful projects, and create an environment where everyone feels motivated and valued. That's what this book is here to help you achieve.

Why IT Management is Unique

So, why is IT management different from managing other teams? For starters, technology never stands still. Every day, there's a new tool, programming language, or workflow to master. The fast pace, combined with the need for precision, means IT managers must balance technical know-how with emotional intelligence and strategic thinking.

In IT, even minor delays or miscommunications can have a significant ripple effect, whether it's a security breach or a service outage. To succeed, you must understand both the technical details and the human side of leadership.

The Impact of Strong IT Management

The IT field stands out from others due to its unique demands and rapid evolution. The persistent pace of technological advancements requires teams to stay flexible and continuously up-to-date with the latest tools, programming languages, and methodologies. This fast-moving environment, paired with the necessity for accuracy, calls for a management style that blends technical expertise with emotional intelligence and strategic vision.

In IT, even minor missteps, such as a miscommunication or slight delay, can escalate quickly. These issues may compromise data security, disrupt system reliability, or diminish customer satisfaction, demonstrating the critical importance of precise coordination and communication. IT managers need to strike a balance: mastering the technical complexities of the field while excelling in the art of managing and motivating people.

Strong management within IT teams leads to measurable improvements across multiple areas:

- **Enhanced Productivity:** Clear goals, streamlined processes, and efficient resource allocation enable teams to work smarter and deliver projects on time.

- **Higher Morale**: A positive work environment where individuals feel appreciated and supported translates into motivated employees who are more invested in the organization's success.

- **Improved Alignment with Business Goals:** When IT teams understand the larger organizational objectives, they're better equipped to deliver solutions that drive business value.

- **Faster Problem-Solving:** A well-coordinated and empowered team can address challenges head-on, resolving issues quickly and minimizing disruptions to operations. Their ability to act swiftly not only keeps systems running smoothly but also strengthens overall team confidence and efficiency.

An IT manager's ability to promote these benefits depends on technical skills, management techniques, and interpersonal abilities. This book is designed to equip you with the knowledge and tools needed to succeed in this dynamic role, providing a balance of theory, practical examples, and visual aids to support your journey.

What You'll Learn

In this book, each chapter dives into a key area of IT team management, equipping readers with tools, frameworks, and templates to apply these concepts in real-world scenarios. Readers will gain insights into building a solid foundation for their teams, understanding team dynamics, structuring IT teams effectively, leveraging personality types, selecting the right members, establishing clear roles and responsibilities, and onboarding new team members.

Leadership styles and strategies are examined in depth, providing an overview of different approaches, guidance on adapting leadership styles to meet team needs, and advice on developing a personal leadership philosophy. Communication and teamwork are pivotal to IT team success, and the book offers techniques for effective communication, promoting open dialogue and feedback, building a collaborative team environment, and addressing conflict resolution through case studies, including issues like unequal workload distribution, cross-departmental conflicts, and cultural differences within a merged IT team.

Performance management and motivation take center stage as readers learn to set goals and expectations using SMART templates, conduct effective performance reviews, and motivate and retain technical talent.

Templates and strategies are provided to streamline these processes. Professional development and growth are also emphasized, with actionable steps for creating learning opportunities, mentoring team members, and planning for succession and career pathing. The book introduces structured development frameworks tailored for various IT roles, including software developers, network engineers, IT support/help desk staff, cybersecurity professionals, data center operators, project managers, and program managers.

The book also addresses navigating challenges and changes, with chapters dedicated to managing organizational and technological shifts, employing change management strategies, and preparing teams for future trends and innovations. Emerging trends in IT management are examined, with actionable advice on adapting to technological advancements and preparing teams to face future challenges. Each chapter is designed to be a practical guide, ensuring readers can implement these strategies effectively in their IT management journey.

CHAPTER 1
BUILDING TEAM DYNAMICS AND ROLE CLARITY

Learn the essentials of team dynamics, including how to select the right team members, set clear roles and responsibilities, and create a solid foundation for collaboration.

Understanding Team Dynamics

In IT, we're lucky to work with teams that bring together a mix of personalities, skills, and experiences. Understanding how these differences impact communication and teamwork is key to helping your team thrive. When we get it right, strong team dynamics ignite creativity and boost productivity. But if we overlook these elements, misalignment can creep in, leading to conflicts, confusion, and a drop in morale.

Recent studies by McKinsey (Hunt, Layton, & Prince, 2015, *Why Diversity Matters*; Hunt, Yee, Prince, & Dixon-Fyle, 2018, *Delivering Through Diversity*) show that teams with diverse backgrounds and skill sets are 35% more likely to outperform less diverse teams. Understanding and leveraging these dynamics can help IT teams collaborate effectively and spark innovation.

The Structure of an IT Team

IT teams typically consist of specialized roles that depend on individual expertise and solid partnership to accomplish their objectives. Common roles within a technical team include:

1. **System Administrator:** The backbone of IT infrastructure, they ensure servers, networks, and systems run smoothly and securely.

2. **Network Engineer:** The architect of connectivity, responsible for designing, implementing, and maintaining robust network systems to ensure reliable communication and data flow.

3. **Database Administrator (DBA):** The guardian of organizational data, tasked with managing databases to ensure information is stored securely, efficiently, and remains accessible at all times.

4. **Help Desk Technician:** The first line of defense in IT support, they troubleshoot and resolve hardware, software, and system-related issues to keep users productive.

5. **DevOps Engineer**: The bridge between development and operations, they streamline workflows through automation, optimize deployment pipelines, and enhance system scalability.

6. **Cybersecurity Specialist**: The shield of IT systems; they defend networks from cyber threats by implementing security measures, monitoring vulnerabilities, and responding to incidents.

7. **Software Developer**: The creator of digital solutions, they design, write, and refine code to build applications or tools that address business needs.

8. **Site Reliability Engineer (SRE)**: The bridge between operations and development, SREs focus on automating infrastructure and improving system reliability through monitoring and incident response.

9. **Project Manager**: The team's navigator, ensuring that projects stay on track, within budget, and aligned with strategic objectives by coordinating efforts across the team.

10. **Quality Assurance (QA) Analyst**: The gatekeeper of performance, they thoroughly test systems and applications to identify bugs and ensure high standards of usability and functionality.

11. **Cloud Architect**: The visionary of cloud-based solutions, they design and oversee scalable, cost-effective, and secure access to cloud resources for the organization.

Datacenter IT Roles

Datacenters play a critical role in IT infrastructure, requiring specialized positions to ensure seamless operations:

1. **Datacenter Technician**: The hands-on expert for servers and hardware, responsible for maintaining physical infrastructure performing routine inspections, troubleshooting, and repairs.

2. **Facilities Engineer:** The custodian of the datacenter environment, managing power, cooling, and fire suppression systems to maintain optimal operating conditions for equipment.

3. **Rack and Stack Engineer:** The organizer of server racks, tasked with installing, configuring, and arranging hardware to maximize space efficiency and maintain proper cabling.

4. **Datacenter Operations Manager:** The leader of daily operations, ensuring compliance with standards, managing incident responses, and overseeing the smooth running of the facility.

5. **Backup and Recovery Specialist:** The safeguard for critical data, ensuring reliable backups and swift recovery in the event of system failures or disasters.

6. **Infrastructure Architect:** The visionary behind datacenter design, creating scalable and efficient systems to support current operations and future growth.

7. **Network Operations Center (NOC) Analyst:** The sentinel of system uptime, monitoring networks in real-time, identifying issues, and resolving problems to prevent downtime.

8. **Logistics Manager:** The coordinator of hardware resources, overseeing procurement, shipping, and inventory to ensure components are available and delivered efficiently.

9. **Logistics Technician:** The mover and tracker of hardware components, ensuring accurate inventory management and timely deployment within the datacenter.

10. **Environmental Health and Safety Specialist:** The guardian of safety standards, ensuring the datacenter complies with environmental and health protocols for a secure working environment.

Maximizing Team Potential Through Personality Types

Understanding your team's personalities can be a game-changer. Tools like Myers-Briggs or DISC assessments give insight into how people communicate, solve problems, and collaborate. Think of it as unlocking hidden talents to create a stronger, more connected team:

- **Detail-Oriented Problem Solvers:** Individuals who excel at analyzing data, spotting inconsistencies, and focusing on precision (e.g., ISTJ in MBTI or "Conscientious" in DISC) might thrive in roles like **Database Administrator, Quality Assurance Analyst**, or **Cybersecurity Specialist**, where attention to detail is critical.

- **Big Picture Thinkers:** People who are visionary and thrive on strategy (e.g., ENTJ in MBTI or "Dominant" in DISC) may be well-suited for leadership positions like IT Manager, Infrastructure Architect, or Project Manager, where long-term planning and decisive action are essential.

- **Collaborative Team Players:** Those who are naturally compassionate, supportive, and focused on harmony (e.g., ENFJ in MBTI or "Steady" in DISC) could excel in roles like **Help Desk Technician, Human Resources IT Liaison**, or **Team Lead**, where promoting relationships and supporting colleagues is key.

- **Innovative Creatives:** Team members who are imaginative and enjoy thinking outside the box (e.g., INFP in MBTI or "Influential" in DISC) might thrive in roles such as **Software Developer, UI/UX Designer**, or **DevOps Engineer**, where creativity and problem-solving merge.

- **Calm Under Pressure:** Individuals who stay composed and resourceful in high-stress situations (e.g., ISTP in MBTI or a balanced mix in DISC) are ideal for roles like **Datacenter**

Technician, NOC Analyst, or **Incident Response Specialist,** where quick decision-making and adaptability are vital.

By understanding each team member's personality and role within the team, managers can create a balanced, productive environment that capitalizes on each individual's strengths while promoting collaboration.

Balancing Technical Work with Management Responsibilities

Transitioning from a hands-on technical role to management can be overwhelming. The key is to delegate effectively and prioritize leadership tasks that align with organizational goals.

Strategies for Balancing Roles

1. **Time Blocking**: Dedicate specific hours for technical tasks and managerial duties. Example: Reserve mornings for team planning and afternoons for technical oversight.
2. **Delegate Wisely**: Assign routine technical work to capable team members. For instance, let a junior technician handle recurring system updates while you focus on strategic projects.
3. **Use Tools to Stay Updated**: Rely on dashboards and monitoring tools (e.g., Nagios for network performance) to stay informed without micromanaging.

Selecting the Right Team Members

Building a strong IT team starts with hiring the right people. Sure, technical chops are important, but they're only part of the picture. It would help if you had people who fit your team's culture. Imagine hiring a coding genius who can't work well with others; that's a recipe for trouble. Instead, look for candidates who are adaptable, great at problem-solving, and genuinely eager to learn. These qualities often turn a good hire into a fantastic one.

1. **Technical Skills**

   Technical expertise is the backbone of any IT role. Look for candidates with relevant certifications, hands-on experience, or a solid educational background. However, remember that technology evolves rapidly. Prioritize individuals who demonstrate a willingness to learn, adapt, and grow with evolving tools and innovations, as this adaptability is just as critical as current technical knowledge.

2. **Soft Skills**

   Interpersonal and communication skills are vital in IT roles, where teamwork and effective problem-solving are key. Seek candidates who:

   - Can clearly and effectively explain complex technical concepts to non-technical audiences.
   - Demonstrate patience and empathy, particularly in customer support or troubleshooting scenarios.
   - Show resilience and composure under pressure, a valuable trait in the fast-paced IT landscape.

Role-Based Hiring

Hiring for specific roles means matching skills with project needs. For example:

- **DevOps Engineers:** Benefit from a blend of development and systems operations skills.
- **Cybersecurity Specialists**: Require up-to-date knowledge of security protocols, ethical hacking, and threat mitigation.

- **Datacenter Technicians**: Need knowledge in hardware maintenance, physical infrastructure troubleshooting, and familiarity with datacenter operations, including power, cabling, and rack management.

Case Study: Hiring for a Technical Support Role

When hiring for a technical support role, look for candidates who combine technical expertise with strong interpersonal skills. The ideal candidate should not only excel at troubleshooting but also demonstrate patience and empathy when assisting users who may have limited IT knowledge. During interviews, ask candidates to describe a time they handled a frustrated user. Pay close attention to how they describe their approach, especially their ability to stay calm, de-escalate tension, and explain technical concepts in a way that's easy to understand.

Establishing Clear Roles and Responsibilities

Clear roles are the glue that holds a team together. When everyone knows their responsibilities, you avoid confusion, missed deadlines, or two people accidentally doing the same task. Imagine starting a project where it's unclear who's handling what; it's chaos waiting to happen. A solid plan keeps everyone on the same page and ensures every task runs smoothly.

The Role of a Team Role Matrix

Do roles on a team start to overlap? That's where a Team Role Matrix can save the day. It breaks down who's responsible for what and highlights where teamwork is needed. For example, your network engineer handles infrastructure, but they'll need to work with your cybersecurity lead to secure it. By mapping out roles this way, everyone knows their lane and how to support each other. For instance, a matrix may include the following:

Role	Key Responsibilities	Cross-Functional Collaboration
Network Engineer	Design and maintain network infrastructure	Works with cybersecurity to secure networks
Developer	Develop and maintain applications	Coordinates with DevOps on deployment
Support Specialist	Provide end-user support and troubleshooting	Works with developers to resolve bugs and improve functionality
Project Manager	Coordinate resources and timelines	Interfaces with all roles for project updates

This matrix helps ensure everyone understands their contributions and who to coordinate with for specific needs.

Onboarding New Team Members

Getting onboarding right can set the stage for your new hire's success. A good plan helps them understand their role, get the tools they need, and feel like part of the team from day one.

Pro Tip: Set up a mentorship program for new hires during their first 90 days. Assigning a buddy not only improves onboarding efficiency but also promotes a sense of belonging.

Onboarding Checklist for New Team Members

Onboarding sets the tone for your new hire's success. A great checklist ensures they're still trying to figure out where to start or who to ask for help. Think of it as a roadmap, covering everything from introducing them to the team to getting their laptop set up. Done right, onboarding makes them feel like they belong from day one.

Sample Onboarding Checklist:

Stage	Tasks	Completed
Pre-Onboarding (Before Start Date)		
Hardware Preparation	Order and configure required devices (e.g., laptop, phone, accessories).	☑
	Install necessary software and tools (e.g., VPN, email client, collaboration tools like Slack or Teams).	☑
System Access	Set up accounts for email, intranet, and other relevant systems.	☑
	Verify permissions align with the new hire's role.	☑
Welcome Email	Include an introduction to the company's culture and values.	☑
	Share the first-day schedule and logistics (e.g., meeting links, office location).	☑
	Provide key contact information, including the manager and mentor/buddy.	☑
Day One (The First Day)		
Introductions	Introduce the new hire to their team during a meeting or informal huddle.	☑
	Schedule a brief meeting with their assigned mentor/buddy to establish a connection.	☑
Access and Documentation	Verify access to all systems and tools.	☑
	Share a welcome kit with:	☑
	- Company policies and procedures.	☑

	- FAQs or a guide for navigating the first few days.	☑
Team Overview	Provide an overview of team responsibilities, workflows, and current projects.	☑
First Week		
Orientation	Conduct sessions on company policies, mission, and vision.	☑
	Provide training on key tools and workflows specific to the role.	☑
Collaboration	Arrange introductory meetings with cross-functional teams the new hire will work with.	☑
Manager Check-In	Have a one-on-one meeting to clarify expectations and short-term goals.	☑
First Month		
Progress and Feedback	Schedule weekly check-ins with the manager to discuss progress and address challenges.	☑
	Provide constructive feedback on initial tasks and celebrate early wins.	☑
Engagement	Assign meaningful tasks and team projects to integrate the new hire into workflows.	☑
Learning Opportunities	Encourage participation in training programs or team meetings to expand knowledge.	☑
First Quarter (First 90 Days)		
Formal Review	Assess performance against the initial goals set during onboarding.	☑
	Identify areas for growth and provide actionable feedback.	☑
Role Adjustment (if needed)	Adjust responsibilities or expectations to align with the new hire's strengths and team needs.	☑

Future Planning	Set long-term goals and discuss career development opportunities within the organization.	☑
Tips for Success	Ensure open communication and encourage the new hire to ask questions.	☑
	Regularly check their comfort level with the pace and complexity of tasks.	☑
	Promote inclusion by involving them in team-building activities or casual gatherings.	☑

Tips for Success

- Ensure open communication and encourage the new hire to ask questions.
- Regularly check their comfort level with the pace and complexity of tasks.
- Promote inclusion by involving them in team-building activities or casual gatherings.

Using an onboarding checklist provides structure, reduces the potential for missed steps, and ensures that new hires receive consistent support as they adapt to their new environment. It also helps them feel confident and equipped to contribute meaningfully to the team.

Closing Remarks

Establishing a strong foundation through understanding team dynamics, selecting the right individuals, clearly defined roles, and an effective onboarding process is essential for building a cohesive and high-performing IT team. These steps not only promote collaboration but also set the tone for future success.

With this groundwork in place, the next chapter will walk you through the shift from technical expertise to leadership. You'll explore strategies to navigate this shift effectively, enabling you to inspire and empower your team while maintaining alignment with organizational goals. Let's dive into the exciting journey of becoming an IT leader.

CHAPTER 2

TRANSITIONING FROM TECHNICAL ROLES TO IT MANAGEMENT

Moving into IT management is an exciting step, but it comes with challenges. This chapter provides practical advice to help you navigate the shift from technical work to strategic leadership.

Introduction: The Leap into Leadership

Moving from a technical role to IT management is a big step. It's exciting, sure, but it can also feel a bit overwhelming. While your technical expertise remains a valuable asset, your focus now shifts. You're no longer just solving problems yourself; you're empowering a whole team to succeed in decision-making and guiding the overall direction. Think of this chapter as your guidebook for navigating this new terrain, helping you build the skills and mindset you need to thrive as an IT manager.

The Key Challenges of Transitioning

1. Shifting from Technical Expert to Strategic Leader

As a technical expert, you were the person everyone turned to when something needed fixing. Now, as a manager, your focus changes. In today's fast-paced IT world, leaders face the challenge of keeping projects aligned with shifting business goals. IT leaders often find themselves juggling daily tasks while trying to stay focused on big-picture goals. That's why it's so important to delegate effectively and set clear priorities. Think of it like moving from playing the game to coaching the team.

Example:

As a systems administrator, Sarah spent her days resolving network issues and maintaining servers. As an IT manager, her focus shifted to planning infrastructure upgrades, negotiating with vendors, and ensuring her team delivered on key performance indicators (KPIs).

2. Delegating Effectively

It's not easy to hand off tasks you know you could handle better or faster yourself, especially when you've been in the trenches for years. However, delegation is key to effective management. For example, instead of troubleshooting a server issue yourself, trust a junior team member to handle it while you focus on a higher-level strategy. Offer guidance, but let them take the lead; it's how both you and your team grow.

Tips for Delegation Success:

- Use tools like Jira, Monday.com, or Trello to assign tasks based on individual strengths and make it easy to track progress. This helps keep everyone accountable without micromanaging.
- Provide clear instructions and set expectations upfront.
- Use regular check-ins to monitor progress without micromanaging.

Example:

John, a newly promoted IT manager, struggled to delegate server maintenance tasks to his junior team members. By creating a structured delegation plan and offering mentorship, he empowered his team while freeing time for strategic responsibilities.

3. Building Leadership Skills

In technical roles, you focus on solving problems and getting things done. Management is a different game; it's about connecting with people, making tough calls, and handling conflicts with grace.

Core Leadership Skills to Develop:

- **Communication:** Conveying expectations clearly and promoting open dialogue.
- **Conflict Resolution:** Addressing disagreements constructively to maintain team harmony.
- **Adaptability:** Adjusting to organizational changes and evolving technologies.

Essential Skills for New IT Managers

Emotional Intelligence: Leading with Empathy

Building trust with your team isn't just about having an open-door policy; it's about showing empathy and understanding what drives them. Emotional intelligence is your secret weapon here. For instance, if a team member seems disengaged, take a moment to check-in. Maybe they're struggling with a project or juggling personal challenges. Being approachable and supportive can make all the difference.

Practical Steps to Improve Emotional Intelligence:

1. Practice active listening in team meetings.
2. Observe nonverbal cues to gauge team morale.
3. Respond to challenges with empathy and patience.

Strategic Thinking: Seeing the Bigger Picture

Strategic thinking enables you to align team efforts with organizational goals. This requires setting long-term objectives, anticipating challenges, and making informed decisions.

Example:

Instead of focusing solely on resolving immediate IT issues, a strategic IT manager would develop a roadmap for transitioning to cloud infrastructure over the next three years.

Delegation: Empowering Your Team

Effective delegation not only lightens your workload but also helps develop your team's skills. Use tools like task management software (e.g., Asana, Trello) to assign and track responsibilities.

Delegation Framework:

1. Identify tasks that can be delegated.
2. Match tasks to team members based on skills and interests.
3. Provide necessary training and resources.

Practical Steps for a Smooth Transition

1. Seek Mentorship

Find a mentor who has successfully transitioned from a technical to a managerial role. They can provide guidance, share lessons learned, and help you navigate challenges.

Example:

Mark, an experienced IT consultant, benefited greatly from shadowing his department head during leadership meetings. This mentorship allowed him to grasp the complexities of team dynamics and organizational strategy.

2. Start Small

Begin by taking on leadership responsibilities in your current role. For example, lead a small project, mentor a junior colleague, or represent your team in cross-departmental meetings.

Case Study:

Before becoming a manager, Lisa led a task force to implement a new ticketing system. This experience honed her leadership skills and built her confidence.

3. Leverage Tools and Resources

Use technology to streamline your transition. Tools like Microsoft Teams, Slack, or Jira can help you manage communication, track progress, and encourage teamwork.

4. Balance Technical and Managerial Tasks

Transitioning doesn't mean abandoning your technical roots. Instead, aim for a balance between hands-on work and managerial duties during the early stages of your new role.

Time Management Tips:

- Dedicate mornings to team planning and afternoons to technical oversight.
- Block off time for professional development activities, such as leadership training.

Path to IT Management Success

Below is a visual roadmap to help you understand the key stages and considerations for transitioning successfully into IT management.

Self-Assessment

Evaluate readiness and skill gaps

Task Delegation

Start delegating technical responsibilities

Skill Development

Enhance leadership and communication abilities

Strategic Focus

Align team goals with organizational priorities

Leadership Ownership

Transition fully into managerial

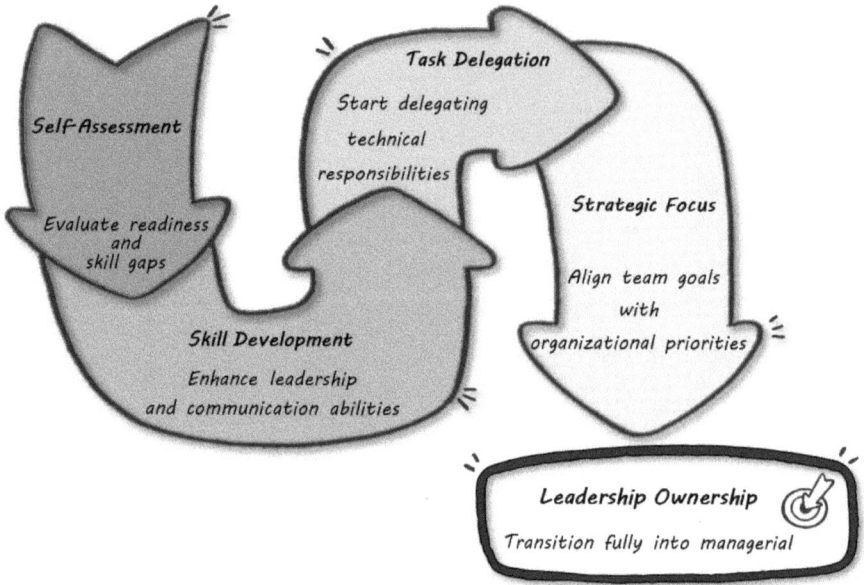

Navigating Common Pitfalls

Pitfall 1: Micromanaging Your Team

Resist the urge to oversee every detail. Instead, trust your team and provide guidance when needed.

Pitfall 2: Overcommitting to Technical Tasks

Avoid spending too much time on technical work at the expense of management responsibilities.

Pitfall 3: Ignoring Team Feedback

Regularly solicit feedback from your team to improve processes and build trust.

Real-World Example: Successful Transitions

Scenario:

Ahmed, a network engineer, struggled to balance his technical expertise with new management responsibilities. By attending leadership workshops and using delegation tools, he successfully led his team through a major infrastructure upgrade.

Case Study: Leading a Remote Team Transition

Background:

Jonathan, a newly promoted IT manager, faced the challenge of leading a remote team during a cloud migration project.

Actions Taken:

1. Scheduled weekly virtual check-ins to ensure alignment.
2. Used project management software to track progress.
3. Encouraged open communication through anonymous feedback surveys.

Outcome:

The project was completed on time, and team morale remained high.

Practical steps for new managers transitioning into leadership roles:

Step	Action	Outcome
Identify Strengths	Reflect on technical expertise and leadership potential.	Confidence in existing skills.
Develop Emotional Intelligence	Practice active listening and empathy-building exercises.	Stronger team rapport.

Learn Delegation	Start delegating small tasks to test team capabilities.	Builds team autonomy.
Seek Mentorship	Identify a mentor to guide the transition.	Gain insights and strategies from experience.
Create Leadership Goals	Set short-term and long-term goals for team management.	Clarity in leadership direction.

Closing Remarks:

Building a strong IT team starts with understanding dynamics, defining roles, and encouraging collaboration. By tapping into your team's diverse strengths and creating an efficient onboarding experience, you can set the stage for innovation and productivity. As you transition from foundational steps to exploring leadership styles, the next chapter will guide you in adapting your approach to maximize team performance and engagement.

CHAPTER 3
LEADERSHIP STYLES AND STRATEGIES

Every IT team is different, which means your leadership style needs to be flexible. This chapter dives into the most effective leadership approaches, helping you adapt to your team's unique needs and drive success.

Overview of Different Leadership Styles

When it comes to leadership, there's no one-size-fits-all approach, especially in IT. Your team could be a mix of seasoned pros and newcomers fresh out of school. The trick is knowing when to adapt your style. If you're dealing with a crisis like a server meltdown, you might need to take charge decisively (that's where an autocratic style comes in). But if you're brainstorming new product features, a democratic approach that taps into everyone's creativity can work wonders.

Example: Transformational leaders inspire their teams to innovate and improve. For example, during a data center transition, a transformational leader might encourage creative solutions to streamline workflows.

Common Leadership Styles and Their Applicability in IT:

1. Transformational Leadership:

- Focus: Inspires team members to innovate and pursue continuous improvement.
- Best For: High-stakes projects, innovation-driven environments, and fast-growing teams.
- **Example:** In a data center transition project, a transformational leader might encourage team members to look into innovative ways to streamline processes and improve efficiency.

2. Transactional Leadership:

- Focus: Based on clear expectations and rewards or penalties.
- Best For: Routine tasks, high compliance requirements, and junior teams needing guidance.

- **Example:** Transactional leadership may be effective for managing help desk teams with strict performance metrics or SLA-based objectives.

3. Servant Leadership:

- Focus: Prioritizes the team's needs and professional growth over personal authority.
- Best For: Teams that require mentorship, strong collaboration, and a supportive environment.
- **Example**: A servant leader in an IT team might prioritize providing the necessary resources, training, and mentorship to help team members excel in their roles.

4. Autocratic Leadership:

- Focus: Centralized control with the leader making most decisions.
- Best For: Crisis situations requiring quick decision-making.
- **Example:** In an unexpected data breach, an autocratic approach may be necessary to ensure immediate, decisive action to protect data integrity.

5. Democratic Leadership:

- Focus: Encourages team input and shared decision-making.
- Best For: Collaborative projects and teams with high levels of expertise.
- **Example:** In a system redesign project, a democratic leader may involve team members in brainstorming sessions to leverage diverse expertise and perspectives.

Leadership Style Comparison Chart:

Leadership Style	Innovation Potential	Adaptability	Control	Collaboration	Team Support
Transformational	★★★★★	★★★★★	★★	★★★★	★★★★
Transactional	★★	★★★	★★★★★	★★	★★★
Servant	★★★★	★★★★	★	★★★★★	★★★★★
Autocratic	★	★★	★★★★★	★	★
Democratic	★★★★	★★★★	★★	★★★★★	★★★★

Explanation of Ratings:

- **Transformational Leadership:** Scores high in flexibility and team empowerment due to its focus on innovation and improvement but is less effective in crisis situations where swift decisions are needed.

- **Transactional Leadership:** In structured environments with clear expectations but has limited flexibility and empowerment.

- **Servant Leadership:** Prioritizes team growth and collaboration, making it highly empowering but less effective in high-pressure or crisis scenarios.

- **Autocratic Leadership:** Best suited for crises requiring immediate action but lacks flexibility and team engagement.

- **Democratic Leadership:** Combines flexibility and team input, making it ideal for collaborative IT environments but less suitable for high-pressure situations.

Manager or Leader: What is the Difference?

The terms "manager" and "leader" are often confused or used synonymously, but they represent different approaches to guiding and inspiring a team. While a manager emphasizes processes, structures, and achieving specific outcomes, a leader focuses on inspiring vision, promoting innovation, and building trust. In IT management, the most effective professionals blend the strengths of both roles, adjusting their approach to meet the needs of the team and the organization. This section examines the differences between managers and leaders, their respective roles in IT, and how to balance these skills for optimal team performance.

Defining Manager vs. Leader

Aspect	Manager	Leader
Focus	Achieving short-term objectives and maintaining operational efficiency.	Inspiring a shared vision and motivating the team toward long-term goals.
Approach	Directive and task-oriented, focused on control and structure.	Empowering and people-oriented, emphasizing trust and teamwork.
Decision-Making	Follows organizational policies and established procedures.	Encourages creative problem-solving and risk-taking.
Motivation Style	Relies on authority, incentives, and performance metrics.	Builds intrinsic motivation through personal connections and shared purpose.
Key Skills	Planning, organizing, budgeting, and monitoring.	Vision-setting, emotional intelligence, innovation, and adaptability.

Key Characteristics of Managers

Managers excel in:

1. Structure and Organization:

- Managers establish clear roles, responsibilities, and workflows, ensuring tasks are executed efficiently.

Example: An IT manager develops a project plan for a data migration project, defining timelines, allocating resources, and monitoring progress.

2. Risk Management:

- Managers identify potential risks and create contingency plans.

  Example: Before implementing a new software system, the manager ensures a rollback strategy is in place to minimize operational disruption.

3. Accountability and Performance:

- Managers track performance metrics and ensure the team meets specific targets.

  Example: An IT manager conducts quarterly reviews to evaluate whether the team meets SLA commitments.

Key Characteristics of Leaders

Leaders stand out in:

1. Vision and Direction:

- Leaders articulate a compelling vision that aligns with organizational goals and inspires teams.

  Example: A leader envisions transitioning to cloud-native solutions and rallies the team around the benefits of scalability and innovation.

2. Empowering Others:

- Leaders focus on developing their team's potential and encouraging autonomy.

Example: An IT leader delegates ownership of a system redesign project to a promising team member, promoting growth and innovation.

3. Adaptability:

- Leaders embrace change and encourage teams to experiment and innovate.

  Example: A leader promotes Agile practices in IT operations to better respond to evolving business needs.

Real-World Examples of Manager vs. Leader in IT

Scenario 1: System Downtime

- **Manager:** Coordinates with the team to troubleshoot and resolve the issue quickly while ensuring incident reports are logged.
- **Leader:** Motivates the team to learn from the downtime, building a culture of resilience and continuous improvement.

Scenario 2: Implementing New Technology

- **Manager:** Ensures the deployment is completed on time and within budget, adhering to a predefined implementation plan.
- **Leader:** Builds excitement around the new technology, emphasizing its potential to transform workflows and enhance innovation.

Scenario 3: Employee Development

- **Manager:** Schedules training programs and monitors participation to ensure skill gaps are addressed.
- **Leader:** Mentors team members, encouraging them to pursue certifications and explore roles that align with their passions.

Balancing Managerial and Leadership Skills

The best IT professionals seamlessly blend management and leadership to navigate complex projects, motivate teams, and achieve strategic goals. Here's how to strike the right balance:

1. Be Task-Oriented Yet Vision-Driven:

- **Managerial Focus:** Ensure tasks are completed on time and meet quality standards.
- **Leadership Lens:** Link everyday tasks to the organization's bigger vision to inspire purpose.

  Example: An IT professional managing an infrastructure upgrade highlights how the project supports the company's innovation strategy.

2. Combine Authority with Empathy:

- **Managerial Approach:** Enforce policies and maintain discipline.
- **Leadership Approach:** Promote open communication and trust, understanding individual team members' motivations.

  Example: While addressing performance issues, an IT manager provides constructive feedback while encouraging the employee to share the challenges they face.

3. Plan Strategically and Adapt Dynamically:

- **Managerial Role:** Use data-driven analysis to create detailed plans and set realistic milestones.
- **Leadership Role:** Remain flexible and adjust plans as circumstances evolve.

Example: A manager plans a software rollout in phases but adapts the timeline based on team feedback during testing.

Leadership and Management in IT Context

When to Act as a Manager:

- **Crisis Management:** During a system outage or security breach, where precise coordination and rapid decision-making are critical.
- **Resource Allocation:** Ensuring team members and tools are optimally distributed for efficiency.

When to Act as a Leader:

- **Cultural Transformation:** Shifting the team to adopt DevOps practices or Agile methodologies.
- **Inspiring Innovation:** Encouraging the team to experiment with emerging technologies like AI and machine learning.

Developing Both Skills

Practical Tips for IT Managers to Build Leadership Skills:

1. **Invest in Emotional Intelligence:** Learn to empathize and build rapport with team members.
2. **Embrace Continuous Learning:** Stay informed about industry trends and innovative management strategies.
3. **Promote Team Collaboration:** Create opportunities for cross-functional engagement to build trust and promote innovation.

Practical Tips for IT Leaders to Build Managerial Skills:

1. **Master Project Management Tools:** Gain proficiency in platforms like Jira, Trello, or Microsoft Project.

2. **Focus on Metrics:** Learn to set KPIs and interpret performance data effectively.

3. **Refine Budgeting Skills:** Understand financial concepts like CapEx and OpEx to align your IT strategies with overall financial goals.

In IT, the question isn't whether to be a manager or a leader; it's when to embody each role. A manager ensures stability and operational efficiency, while a leader drives innovation and inspires growth. By mastering both, IT professionals can build a high-performing, motivated, and adaptable team ready to address today's challenges and tomorrow's opportunities.

Adapting Leadership Style to Team Needs

One of the most valuable skills an IT manager can possess is the ability to adapt their leadership style to the current needs of the team and project. Flexibility enables a manager to lead effectively across different situations, whether the goal is to inspire a team through innovation or ensure strict compliance during regulatory audits.

Practical Tips for Adapting Leadership Style:

- **Identify the Team's Needs:** Evaluate the team's strengths, weaknesses, experience levels, and project requirements. For example, a newly formed team might benefit from a more structured, transactional approach initially.

- **Evaluate Project Phases:** Shift styles as the project evolves. For instance, during the brainstorming phase, democratic leadership may work well, but as the project nears completion, a more directive approach could help meet deadlines.

- **Assess Team Feedback:** Regular feedback from team members can reveal when they may benefit from more autonomy or when additional guidance is needed.

Real-World Example: In a hardware migration project, an IT manager might begin with a democratic leadership style, encouraging the team to provide insights on potential risks and compatibility challenges. As the migration progresses, they could transition to a transformational approach, inspiring the team to overcome obstacles and find innovative solutions to unexpected issues. In the final phase, a transactional style may be employed to enforce strict adherence to testing procedures and compliance with deployment protocols and ensure all hardware components meet performance standards, guaranteeing a smooth and successful migration.

Developing a Personal Leadership Philosophy

A personal leadership philosophy guides decision-making, helps establish a manager's unique identity, and creates consistency in how they lead. Your leadership philosophy is like your personal playbook; it reflects your values and guides how you manage. Think back to moments in your career when you felt inspired by a leader or frustrated by poor management. What did you learn from those experiences? Use that insight to define how you want to lead your team.

Pro Tip: Write your core leadership principles and revisit them monthly. Tools like BetterUp and Humantelligence offer AI-driven coaching to help refine leadership philosophies based on team feedback.

Steps to Develop a Leadership Philosophy:

1. **Identify Core Values:** Reflect on values like integrity, innovation, teamwork, and accountability, which should guide your decisions and interactions.

2. **Define Your Mission:** Think about your ultimate goal as a leader – is it to develop future leaders, promote innovation, or achieve operational excellence?

3. **Create a Consistent Approach:** Outline key principles, such as maintaining transparency, prioritizing team development, or encouraging open communication.

Example: A manager focused on empowerment might adopt a philosophy centered on servant leadership with a mission to support and grow team members' skills. They might prioritize transparency, frequently share performance insights, and encourage continuous learning.

Pro Tip: Write down your core leadership principles and review them monthly. This practice keeps your philosophy aligned with evolving team and organizational goals.

Decision-Making Framework

Below is a visual guide to streamline decision-making processes, ensuring consistency and alignment with team and organizational goals.

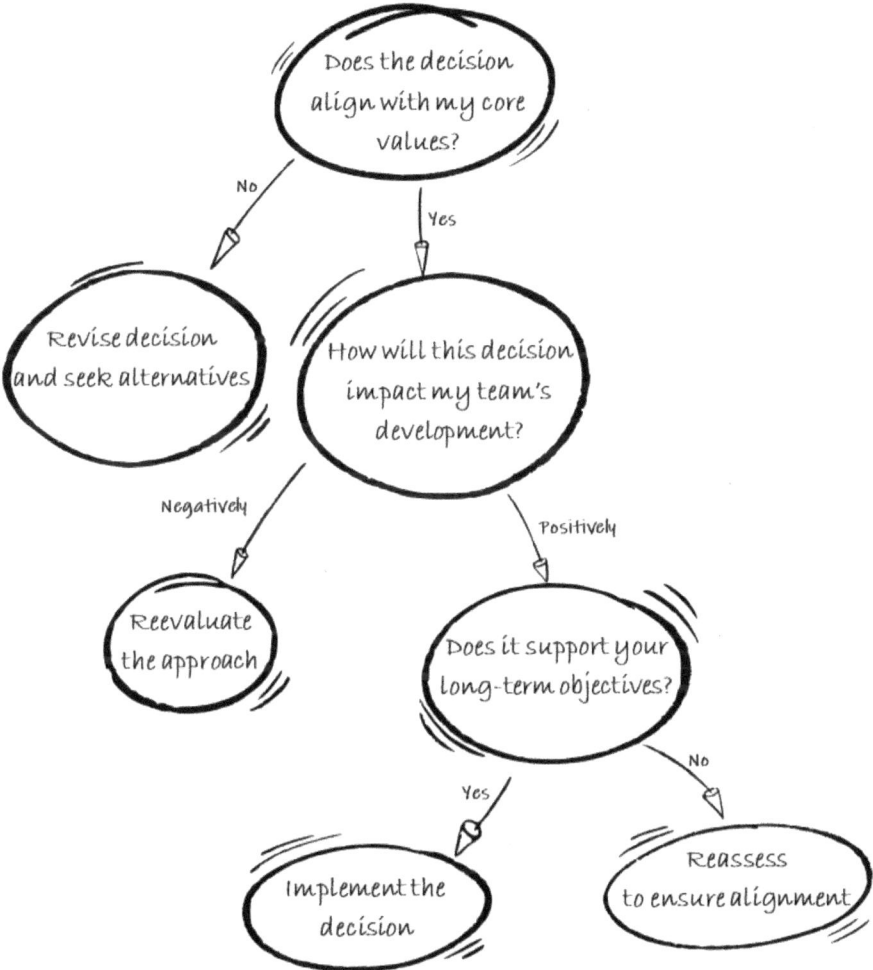

When leaders consistently follow their personal philosophy, they build trust within their teams, making their decisions appear fair, thoughtful, and aligned with team goals.

Techniques for Effective Communication

Effective communication is the backbone of successful IT team management. Given the complexity of technical projects and the range of stakeholders involved, clear and purposeful communication can prevent misunderstandings, speed up problem resolution, and strengthen team cohesion. In this section, we'll examine techniques that enable managers to convey complex information, promote open dialogue, and create a collaborative atmosphere.

Best Practices for Technical Communication:

- **Use Clear, Concise Language:** Simplify technical jargon, especially when speaking to non-technical stakeholders. Clarity and brevity help prevent information overload and improve understanding.

- **Provide Context:** Always set the stage with background information, such as why a particular decision was made or the impact of a technical issue on business goals.

- **Confirm Understanding:** Encourage feedback, ask clarifying questions, and summarize key points to ensure everyone is on the same page.

- **Adapt to Your Audience:** Tailor your communication style to different audiences, executives, team members, or external stakeholders, focusing on their needs and levels of technical familiarity.

Example: When presenting a network performance update to executive leadership, an IT manager might highlight the impact of overall service reliability on business operations and customer satisfaction rather than delving into the technical specifics of individual metrics.

Communication Flowchart

This flowchart outlines the key steps to ensure clear, concise, and effective communication across all levels of your IT team.

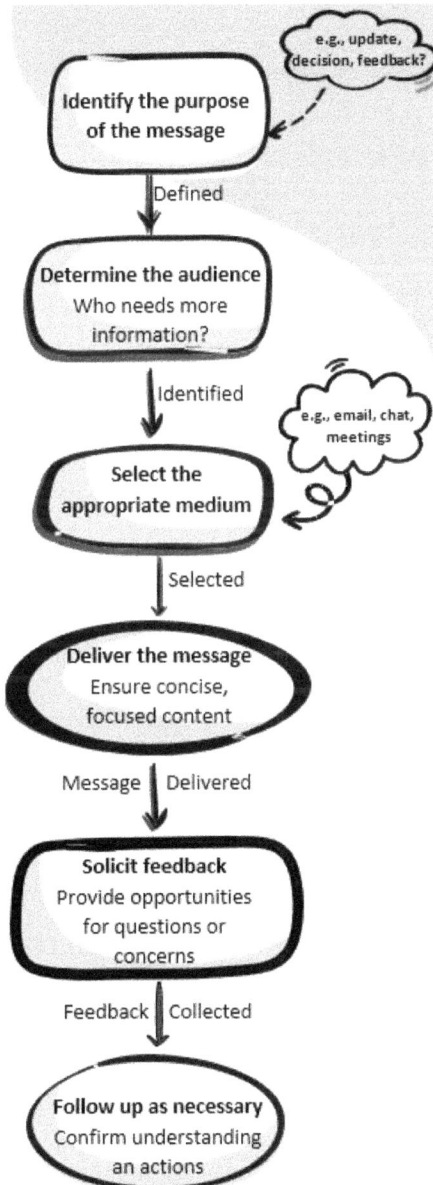

Identify the purpose of the message

e.g., update, decision, feedback?

Defined

Determine the audience
Who needs more information?

Identified

e.g., email, chat, meetings

Select the appropriate medium

Selected

Deliver the message
Ensure concise, focused content

Message Delivered

Solicit feedback
Provide opportunities for questions or concerns

Feedback Collected

Follow up as necessary
Confirm understanding an actions

Encouraging Open Dialogue and Feedback

Creating an environment where team members feel confident sharing insights, concerns, and feedback is essential for building an engaged and high-performing IT team. Managers can promote open dialogue by practicing transparent communication, actively seeking feedback, and creating a culture where diverse opinions are valued and respected. By demonstrating approachability and encouraging regular discussions, leaders can strengthen trust, collaboration, and overall team effectiveness.

Strategies for Encouraging Open Communication

1. **Regular Check-Ins:** Hold weekly or bi-weekly one-on-one meetings with team members to discuss project progress, address any obstacles, and gather feedback.

2. **Team Retrospectives:** After each project or major milestone, organize a retrospective to discuss what went well and areas for improvement. Emphasize constructive feedback and focus on continuous improvement.

3. **Anonymous Feedback Channels:** Provide options like surveys or suggestion boxes for team members to share honest feedback without fear of reprisal.

Real-World Insight: In a weekly team meeting, an IT manager might ask open-ended questions such as, "What challenges are you currently facing?" or "How can we improve our process?" These prompts encourage team members to share openly, paving the way for a more collaborative environment.

Feedback Loop Diagram

This diagram highlights how to establish a continuous feedback loop, promoting open dialogue, improvement, and trust within your team.

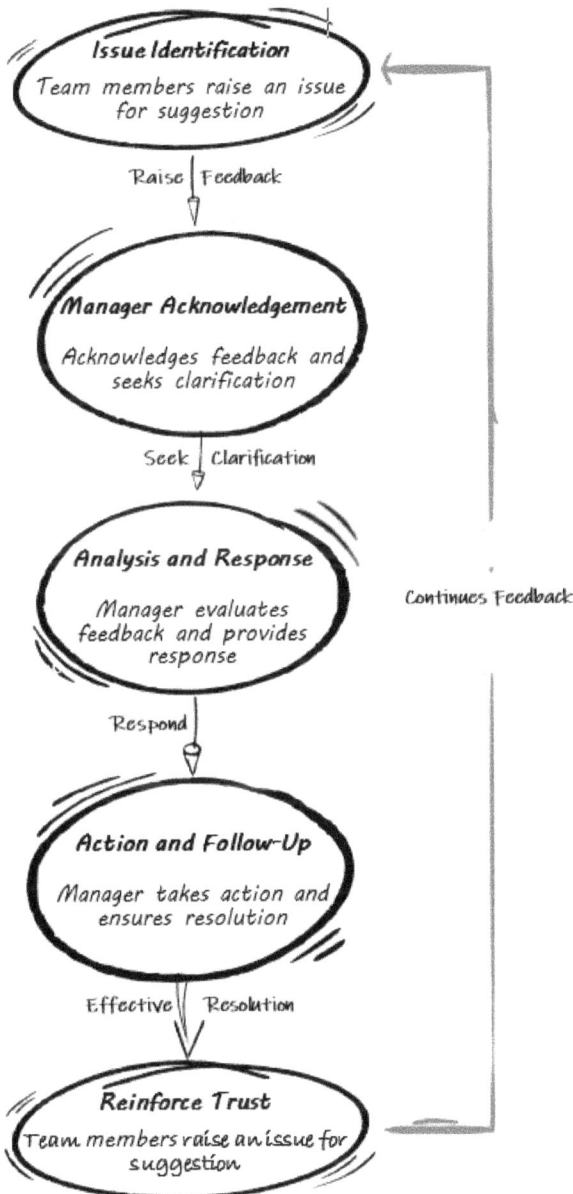

Building a Collaborative Team Environment

Collaboration is essential for IT teams handling complex tasks and projects that require diverse skill sets. Effective teamwork relies on a supportive environment, where team members work together towards shared goals, leveraging each other's strengths. Managers play a critical role in setting up structures and processes that enable efficient cooperation.

Key Elements of a Collaborative Environment

1. **Defined Communication Channels:** Use designated channels for different types of communication, such as email for formal updates, messaging apps for quick interactions, and video conferencing for team discussions.

2. **Collaboration Tools:** Equip the team with tools like project management software (e.g., Asana, Trello), code collaboration platforms (e.g., GitHub), and document sharing tools (e.g., Google Drive) to facilitate smooth workflows.

3. **Cross-Functional Meetings:** Regularly hold meetings that bring together different departments or specialties to encourage cross-functional knowledge-sharing and problem-solving.

4. **Clear Project Roles and Responsibilities:** Ensure that each team member understands their role in each project, as well as how their work connects with the contributions of others.

Example: In a system upgrade project, a collaborative team environment might include regular standup meetings, a shared project management board, and designated channels for both technical and operational discussions. This setup encourages transparency, ensures everyone is aligned, and minimizes redundant efforts.

Communication and Collaboration Flowchart

This flowchart illustrates the essential pathways for effective communication and teamwork within your team, promoting efficient workflows and stronger connections.

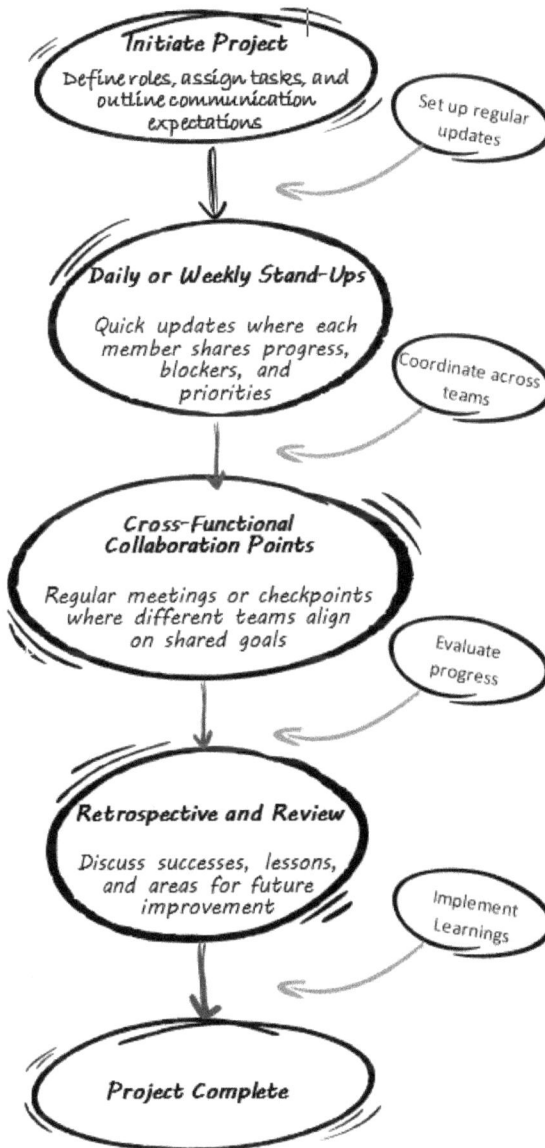

Closing Remarks

Adjusting your leadership style to fit your team's needs is key for success in IT management. Whether you're inspiring new ideas, keeping things organized, or guiding through challenges, good leadership means knowing when to take charge and when to work together. This balance helps your team perform at their best. As you continue building your leadership skills, the next chapter will cover ways to handle conflicts and create a strong problem-solving mindset within your IT team.

CHAPTER 4

CONFLICT RESOLUTION AND PROBLEM-SOLVING

Conflict is a natural part of any team dynamic, especially in technical environments where priorities, deadlines, and differing approaches often clash. This chapter explores strategies to identify, mediate, and resolve conflicts while promoting a culture of constructive problem-solving within IT teams.

Conflict is a natural part of any team dynamic, especially in technical environments where priorities, deadlines, and differing approaches often clash. This chapter explores strategies to identify, mediate, and resolve conflicts while promoting a culture of constructive problem-solving within IT teams. By expanding with in-depth examples, case studies, and actionable insights, this chapter aims to equip managers and team members with practical tools.

Pro Tip: Use anonymous surveys to identify underlying tensions within the team. Tools like Google Forms or Typeform can encourage honesty and reveal areas for improvement.

Identifying Sources of Conflict

Conflicts don't just appear out of nowhere; they have roots. It could be conflicting priorities, miscommunications, or personality clashes. The key is to spot these issues early before they escalate. For instance, if you notice your developers and security team clashing over deadlines, it's time to step in and get everyone back on the same page before tensions rise.

Common Sources of Conflict in IT Teams

1. **Resource Allocation:** In remote teams, communication gaps are one of the biggest sources of conflict. According to Buffer's *State of Remote Work 2023* report, 20% of remote teams face challenges with misaligned priorities. This highlights just how important it is to have clear processes in place and regular alignment meetings to keep everyone on the same page.

   - **Example:** A development team needed high-performance servers for testing, but the infrastructure team had allocated those servers to another department. This led to delays and friction. Implementing a clear resource scheduling system resolved the issue.

- **In-depth Insight:** Shared resources can sometimes expose inefficiencies in how infrastructure is planned. To address this, teams can use capacity forecasting models to predict busy times and plan resource allocation ahead of time.

2. **Competing Priorities:** Differences in goals, such as developers focusing on innovation while security teams prioritize risk reduction, often result in clashes.

   - **Case Study:** A security team delayed a product launch due to vulnerability concerns, causing tension with developers eager to meet the deadline. Through mediation, they agreed on a phased rollout addressing critical vulnerabilities first.

   - **Real-World Expansion:** In some organizations, forming a cross-functional team for critical launches helps keep everyone on the same page. These teams strike a balance between pushing for innovation and maintaining operational stability, reducing potential conflicts along the way.

3. **Technical Disagreements:** Strong opinions about tools, methods, or programming approaches can create tension.

   - **Example:** A debate over which database technology to use for a critical project was resolved by evaluating objective performance metrics, leading to a consensus.

   - **Further Context:** Formal technical discussions, paired with peer reviews and thorough risk assessments, transform disagreements into valuable opportunities for collaborative growth and learning.

4. **Personality Clashes:** Diverse personalities enrich a team but can lead to misunderstandings or interpersonal tension.

   - **Case Study:** A team experienced interpersonal conflict between a detail-oriented project manager and a results-driven engineer.

Personality assessments and team-building exercises improved understanding and teamwork.

- **Expanded View:** Promoting a shared accountability model helps build mutual respect, encouraging individuals to prioritize shared goals over personal differences.

5. **Workload Distribution:** Unequal workloads, particularly between senior and junior team members, can cause frustration and disengagement.

- **Insight:** Rotating responsibilities and setting clear workload expectations during sprint planning sessions help mitigate such issues.

- **Example in Depth:** A mentorship-driven workload allocation where juniors shadow senior roles periodically builds expertise while reducing bottlenecks on high-stakes tasks.

Mediating and Resolving Conflicts

Effective conflict resolution involves structured steps that promote understanding, collaboration, and alignment on shared goals.

Steps for Effective Conflict Resolution:

1. **Recognize and Address the Issue Early:** Encourage team members to raise concerns promptly.

- **Case Study:** In a development sprint, unresolved disagreements over code quality standards delayed progress. Early intervention through daily standups helped identify the issue and prevent further delays.

2. **Understand Both Perspectives:** Facilitate discussions where everyone's viewpoint is heard.

- **Real-World Insight:** Active listening practices, such as mirroring team members' concerns, help create an environment of trust, enabling solutions.

3. **Identify Common Goals:** Focus on shared objectives to shift the narrative from personal differences to team success.

    - **Example:** In a project involving UX designers and backend engineers, aligning on customer satisfaction as the primary goal resolved disagreements over design complexity.

4. **Develop a Solution Together:** Collaborate to create solutions that respect differing perspectives.

    - **Case Study:** In a data center, operational teams collaborated with development teams to create deployment schedules that balanced stability and innovation, leading to better project outcomes.

5. **Follow-Up:** Ensure the agreed-upon solution is implemented effectively and all parties are satisfied.

    - **Detailed Analysis:** Continuous feedback loops via post-resolution surveys strengthen long-term team dynamics and prevent the recurrence of similar issues.

Pro Tip: *During mediation, focus on framing the issue as a team problem rather than an individual one. This approach reduces defensiveness and promotes teamwork.*

Tools and Techniques for Conflict Resolution

Conflict Resolution Flowchart

This flowchart visually represents the steps and techniques for resolving conflicts effectively, helping teams identify root causes and work together on lasting solutions.

Identify Issue

Acknowledge and define the conflict

Define conflict

Listen to Prospectives

Facilitate discussion of viewpoints

Share Prospectives

Find Common Ground

Emphasize shared goals and values

Align Goals

Develop a Resolution

Agree on a course of action·

Agree on Actions

Implement & Follow Up

Execute the solution and check in to confirm satisfaction

Confirm Resolution

Resolution Achieved

Expanded Tools:

1. **Mediation Sessions:** Use neutral facilitators to guide discussions for high-tension conflicts.

   - **Example:** Bringing in a third-party mediator helped resolve tension in a large-scale system migration project, where blame-shifting between teams had stalled progress.

2. **Surveys and Feedback Tools:** Collect anonymous feedback to understand team concerns and uncover hidden conflicts.

   - **Case Study:** A feedback survey revealed dissatisfaction among remote team members about communication gaps, leading to the implementation of a weekly virtual town hall.

3. **Behavioral Assessments:** Use tools like DISC or MBTI to understand personality clashes and improve team dynamics.

   - **In-depth Usage:** Pairing complementary personality types in mentorship programs accelerates collaboration in high-pressure scenarios.

Promoting a Culture of Problem-Solving

Problem-solving is an essential skill in IT, where unexpected challenges are the norm. A problem-solving culture starts with you. If you show your team that it's okay to experiment and learn from mistakes, they'll feel confident tackling challenges head-on. For instance, when a junior team member proposes a fix for a recurring bug, support their initiative, even if it doesn't work the first time. That encouragement builds a culture of innovation and ownership.

Strategies to Promote Problem-Solving:

1. **Encourage Proactive Thinking:** Emphasize that all team members should seek solutions rather than waiting for instructions.

   - **Example:** A database administrator's proactive automation of daily backups reduced operational risks by 30%.

2. **Implement Problem-Solving Frameworks:** Utilize models like Root Cause Analysis, Fishbone Diagrams, or 5 Whys to diagnose issues systematically.

   - **Case Study:** A root cause analysis of recurring deployment failures revealed gaps in the testing process. By implementing automated pre-deployment tests, the team significantly reduced errors, improving overall project reliability and delivery timelines.

3. **Reward Initiative:** Recognize and reward team members who identify and resolve problems.

   - **Example:** A quarterly award for innovative solutions inspired a team to implement predictive analytics, saving downtime costs.

4. **Facilitate Knowledge Sharing:** Organize sessions where team members present recent problems, they've solved to promote collective learning.

   - *Expanded Practice:* Knowledge-sharing platforms like Confluence or Miro ensure these learnings are preserved for future use.

Root Cause Analysis Table

Problem	Root Cause	Solution
High system downtime	Server overload	Increase server capacity and optimize load
Delayed project timelines	Misaligned expectations	Improve project scoping and planning
Frequent code errors	Lack of QA procedures	Implement code reviews and QA processes

Detailed root cause analyses, including failure logs and stakeholder interviews, uncover systemic issues otherwise overlooked.

Conflict Resolution and Problem-Solving in Practice

Real-World Examples:

1. **Conflict Over Unequal Workload Distribution:**
   - Junior developers expressed dissatisfaction with repetitive tasks, while senior developers felt overwhelmed. Implementing a mentorship program and rotating responsibilities balanced the workload and improved morale.

2. **Innovative Problem-Solving:**
   - During a server outage, a technician identified and resolved airflow issues, preventing further disruptions. Recognizing such initiatives encourages a proactive culture.

3. **Complex Team Dynamics:**
   - A team dealing with cross-departmental projects faced communication gaps. Weekly alignment meetings bridged understanding and improved teamwork.

4. **Escalating Issues:**

- A conflict between two team leaders over resource allocation escalated to senior management. Mediation uncovered the root cause —misaligned project priorities— and implementing a clearer resource allocation plan resolved the conflict.

Conflict Resolution Tools

Tool	What It Does	When to Use It	How It Helps
Mediation Sessions	Facilitates neutral discussion for resolution	When tension between teams is persistent	Uncovers the root cause and builds common ground
Root Cause Analysis	Diagnoses recurring issues systematically	When a problem keeps coming back	Identifies underlying causes to prevent future conflicts
Anonymous Surveys	Collects unfiltered feedback	When team members are reluctant to speak up	Highlights unseen tensions or morale issues
Behavioral Assessments	Improves team understanding	When personality clashes affect teamwork	Aligns roles with strengths and communication styles

Closing Remarks

Conflict is inevitable in IT environments but, when managed effectively, can lead to stronger teams and innovative solutions. By identifying root causes, mediating disputes constructively, and building a problem-solving culture, you can turn challenges into growth opportunities. With structured frameworks and a collaborative approach, your team will develop the resilience to navigate conflicts smoothly. In the next chapter, you'll learn about performance management and motivation, critical tools for sustaining high-performing teams.

CHAPTER 5
PERFORMANCE MANAGEMENT AND MOTIVATION

Dive into performance management, including goal-setting, conducting reviews, and motivational techniques specific to technical talent.

Setting Goals and Expectations

Clear, achievable goals are crucial for aligning your team's work with the organization's big-picture objectives. Think of goals as a roadmap; they guide your team and keep everyone focused on where you're headed. With them, projects can easily stay on course. So, set specific, measurable targets to give your team a clear sense of purpose and progress. For example, rather than saying "improve system performance", set a goal like "reduce server response time by 20% over the next quarter.". In IT teams, where projects often involve complex tasks and multiple dependencies, well-defined goals ensure that every team member understands their role and contributions to the bigger picture.

Principles for Effective Goal Setting:

1. **Align with Organizational Goals:** Team goals should reflect broader company objectives to ensure everyone works toward the same end.

2. **Use SMART Goals:** SMART (Specific, Measurable, Achievable, Relevant, Time-bound) criteria provide a framework for setting goals that are clear and actionable.

3. **Involve Team Members:** Engage team members in setting goals to boost motivation and accountability.

4. **Set Both Short-Term and Long-Term Goals:** Balance immediate objectives with longer-term career and skill development goals.

Example: A SMART goal for a network engineer might be, "Reduce network downtime by 20% over the next quarter by implementing automated monitoring and alerting systems." This goal is specific (reducing downtime), measurable (by 20%), achievable (through automation), relevant (supports reliability), and time-bound (by the end of the quarter).

Pro Tip: *Involve team members in defining their goals during one-on-one meetings. This ensures alignment with personal aspirations and organizational objectives.*

A SMART Goal Template can guide IT managers in setting clear and achievable goals with the SMART (Specific, Measurable, Achievable, Relevant, Time-bound) framework:

Example SMART Goal Template Layout:

Goal	Specifics	Measurable Criteria	Achievability Factors	Relevance	Time Frame
Improve ticket response time	Respond in <1 hr	Track via response logs	Sufficient staff, tools	High priority	3 months

Conducting Effective Performance Reviews

Regular performance reviews are critical for providing feedback, setting new goals, and supporting career growth. When done effectively, reviews can boost morale, clarify expectations, and strengthen the manager-team member relationship.

Steps for Conducting Performance Reviews:

1. **Prepare in Advance:** Gather data on the team member's accomplishments, challenges, and overall performance metrics.

2. **Use a Structured Format:** Follow a consistent structure that includes reviewing past goals, discussing achievements, and setting future targets.

3. **Balance Feedback:** Provide both positive feedback and constructive criticism. Acknowledge accomplishments, but also address areas for improvement.

4. **Set Future Goals:** Based on the review, outline goals for the upcoming period and discuss any necessary support or training.

Example: During a performance review with a software developer, an IT manager could start by discussing recent project successes, then suggest areas for skill development (e.g., learning a new programming language), and set a goal for the next quarter.

Pro Tip: *Use a "start-stop-continue" framework during reviews. Ask team members what they should start doing, stop doing, and continue doing to improve their performance.*

Performance Review Template

Creating a performance review template helps maintain consistency and structure. Here's an example:

Performance Area	Review Notes
Accomplishments	Key projects and goals achieved
Areas for Improvement	Skills or behaviors needing development
Future Goals	SMART goals for the upcoming period
Development Support	Training or resources required

Here's another way the template could be organized.

Performance Area	Evaluation	Comments
Key Projects Completed	Exceeds Expectations	Completed migration ahead of schedule.

| Adherence to Timelines | Meets Expectations | Needs slight improvement on long-term tasks. |
| Innovation | Below Expectations | Requires proactive involvement in ideation. |

KPI Tracking Dashboard

Tracking Key Performance Indicators (KPIs) helps align team efforts with organizational goals. Here's an example of a tracking dashboard:

KPI	Baseline	Current	Target	Notes
SLA Adherence (%)	85%	90%	95%	Improved response times
Project Deadlines Met	70%	80%	90%	Monitoring active projects
Employee Engagement	78%	84%	90%	New initiatives in place

Pro Tip: *Use visualization tools like Tableau or Power BI for real-time updates.*

Actionable metrics for tracking IT team performance example:

Metric	Purpose	Calculation Example
SLA Adherence Rate	Measure uptime and service reliability.	(Number of SLAs Met / Total SLAs) x 100%
Team Utilization Rate	Assess workload distribution.	(Billable Hours / Total Hours) x 100%
Mean Time to Resolution (MTTR)	Evaluate efficiency in issue resolution.	Total Downtime / Number of Incidents
Employee Retention Rate	Track talent retention.	(Employees Retained / Starting Employees) x 100%
Training Completion Rate	Monitor skill-building progress.	(Completed Training / Planned Training) x 100%

Performance Review Template Examples

This template provides a structured approach to conducting performance reviews. It focuses on key performance areas, achievements, areas for improvement, and future goal setting. It encourages open communication between managers and employees to promote continuous growth and alignment with team and organizational goals.

Employee Information

- **Employee Name:** _____
- **Job Title:** _____
- **Department:** _____
- **Manager Name:** _____
- **Review Period:** _____

1. Performance Areas

Performance Area	Evaluation	Comments
Key Projects Completed	Review the employee's completion and quality of key projects.	_____ _____ _____
Adherence to Timelines	Evaluate how well the employee met deadlines.	_____ _____ _____
Teamwork	Assess contributions to team cohesion and collaboration.	_____ _____ _____

Innovation	Review the employee's ability to innovate or suggest improvements.	_____ _____ _____

2. Achievements

Achievement	Description
Specific Successes	List key accomplishments during the review period. E.g., successfully completed project X, led initiative Y, or implemented a new process.
Contributions to Team Goals	Describe how the employee's achievements supported overall team or company objectives.

Pro Tip: *Implement micro-rewards for ongoing achievements, such as e-gift cards or shoutouts in team chats, to keep morale consistently high.*

3. Areas for Improvement

Area for Improvement	Development Focus
Identify skills or behaviors needing enhancement	E.g., technical skills, communication, leadership, etc. Focus on providing actionable feedback and suggestions for improvement.

4. Goal Setting

- **Short-Term Goals (Next Quarter)**: Define specific, measurable goals for the next quarter.
- **Long-Term Goals (Annual)**: Outline broader goals for the upcoming year that align with career growth and team objectives.
- **Development Resources or Training Required**: Identify resources, courses, or certifications supporting these goals.

5. Manager Feedback

- **Overall Performance Summary**: Provide constructive comments summarizing the employee's overall performance, strengths, and contributions.

- **Constructive Feedback**: Highlight areas for improvement in a positive, actionable way.

6. Employee Feedback

- **Employee's Comments**: Allow employees to share their thoughts on their performance, feedback, and goals.

7. Final Notes and Signatures

Manager's Signature: _____ Date: _____

Employee's Signature: _____ Date: _____

Note: This template should be used as a guiding tool to encourage meaningful discussion and set clear expectations for future performance. Both parties are encouraged to keep a copy for reference throughout the next review period.

Recommended Tools/Software

Equip your team with tools that streamline processes and enhance efficiency. Here's a comparison of popular IT infrastructure monitoring and security tools:

Category	Tool	Purpose	Pricing
Monitoring	Splunk	Data-driven observability and logging	Enterprise
Monitoring	Datadog	AI-driven real-time infrastructure monitoring	Subscription
Monitoring	Nagios	Real-time infrastructure monitoring	Open Source
Monitoring	Zabbix	Automated performance tracking	Free/Enterprise
Security	CrowdStrike Falcon	Endpoint protection with AI threat detection	Subscription
Security	AIOps Platforms	Automated incident detection and response	Variable Pricing
Security	Snort	Intrusion detection and prevention	Open Source

Modern tools like Datadog and AIOps platforms provide predictive analytics and automated responses, significantly reducing downtime and enhancing operational efficiency.

Pro Tip: *Start with open-source tools to minimize costs during proof-of-concept phases.*

Motivating and Retaining Technical Talent

In the IT industry, where skilled professionals are in high demand, motivating and retaining technical talent is crucial. Understanding what drives your team members and creating a supportive environment can lead to higher satisfaction, loyalty, and performance.

Strategies for Motivation:

1. **Recognize Individual and Team Achievements:** Regularly acknowledge hard work and successes, whether through verbal praise, awards, or public recognition.

2. **Provide Opportunities for Growth:** Offer avenues for professional development, such as certifications, workshops, or conferences.

3. **Encourage Project Ownership:** Empower team members to take responsibility for their projects, allowing them autonomy and decision-making authority.

4. **Build a Positive Team Culture:** Promote a culture where team members feel valued, supported, and encouraged to share ideas.

Real-World Insight: Recognizing a system administrator's contributions in reducing downtime can increase their sense of value, motivating them to continue innovating in their role. Additionally, encouraging them to pursue relevant certifications shows investment in their professional growth.

Motivation Strategy Table

Motivation Strategy	When to Use	Example
Public Recognition	For major achievements	Acknowledging accomplishments in team meetings
Professional Development	When team members want to advance skills	Sponsoring a cybersecurity certification
Project Ownership	For experienced team members	Allowing a developer to lead a project
Positive Feedback	For ongoing tasks and daily efforts	Giving specific praise in one-on-one meetings

By listing different motivational strategies and when to use them can help managers choose the right approach for each team member.

Closing Remarks

Managing performance and keeping your team motivated are key to building a successful IT team. By setting clear goals, providing constructive feedback, and recognizing hard work, you create an environment where people feel valued and driven to succeed. The right mix of structure and support helps your team not just meet expectations but consistently raise the bar. With these practices in place, the next chapter will dive into how to help your team grow through professional development and mentorship opportunities.

CHAPTER 6

PROFESSIONAL DEVELOPMENT AND GROWTH

Equip your team for growth through professional development plans, mentorship programs, and career pathing.

Creating Learning and Development Opportunities

In the ever-evolving world of IT, continuous learning isn't just a nice-to-have; it's a must. New technologies and methodologies pop up all the time. Investing in your team's professional development boosts their skills and Adaptability and increases job satisfaction. And let's be honest: when people feel they're growing, they're more likely to stick around.

Building a Development Plan:

1. **Identify Skills Gaps:** Evaluate each team member's current skill set and identify gaps relevant to their role or future projects.

2. **Set Development Goals:** Create clear goals around skill acquisition, such as learning a new coding language or mastering a specific tool.

3. **Allocate Resources:** Provide access to training resources, courses, or certifications that align with each person's role and aspirations.

4. **Encourage Knowledge Sharing:** Organize knowledge-sharing sessions where team members can share insights from their learning experiences.

Example: A development plan for a cybersecurity analyst might include a goal to earn a Certified Information Systems Security Professional (CISSP) certification within the next year, along with access to relevant study resources.

Pro Tip: *Platforms like LinkedIn Learning and Pluralsight offer personalized learning paths, making it easier for team members to quickly build skills in areas like IT infrastructure and cybersecurity.*

Certification and Learning Pathways

Certifications can provide credibility, improve skills, and open doors for IT professionals aiming for leadership roles. The following table highlights certifications and skills relevant to IT managers:

Certification	Skill Area	Recommended Timeline	Prerequisites
ITIL Foundation	IT Service Management	3 months	Basic IT knowledge
Certified Scrum Master	Agile Methodologies	3 months	None
CISSP	Cybersecurity	6 months	5 years of experience
Microsoft Azure Solutions	Cloud Management	4 months	Familiarity with cloud tech
PMP (Project Management)	Project Leadership	4 months	Project experience

Certifications are constantly evolving to keep up with the ever-changing IT landscape. Take the 2024 CISSP, for example; new modules now focus on AI-driven security protocols to address today's modern cybersecurity challenges.

Pro Tip: *Start with certifications that align with your current role and gradually expand into leadership-focused paths.*

Development Plan Example Template

This template can guide managers in structuring a team member's development plan:

1. Team Member Details

Name: _____

Role/Position: _____

Department: _____

Manager: _____

Date of Plan Initiation: _____

Review Date: _____

2. Development Goals

Clearly define the objectives for the team member's growth and development.

Short-Term Goals (3-6 months):

1. [Specific, measurable goal] _____
2. [Specific, measurable goal] _____

Long-Term Goals (6-12 months):

1. [Specific, measurable goal] _____
2. [Specific, measurable goal] _____

3. Skills Assessment

Identify current strengths and areas for improvement.

Strengths:

- [Skill or trait 1] _____
- [Skill or trait 2] _____

Areas for Improvement:

- [Skill or trait 1] _____
- [Skill or trait 2] _____

4. Action Plan

Outline the specific actions, resources, and support needed to achieve development goals.

Development Activity	Goal Addressed	Deadline	Resources/Support Needed
e.g., Training Program	Short/Long-term	Date	Budget, Mentorship, etc.
e.g., Job Shadowing	Short/Long-term	Date	Collaboration with...
e.g., Project Assignment	Short/Long-term	Date	Tools, Team Support...

5. Milestones and Metrics

Define how progress will be measured.

Key Milestones:

1. [Milestone and target date]_____
2. [Milestone and target date]_____

Metrics for Success:

e.g., Completion of a course, improvement in KPIs

6. Manager's Support

Outline how the manager will support the team member in achieving their goals.

Regular Check-Ins: [e.g., Weekly, bi-weekly]

Feedback Mechanisms: [e.g., 360-degree feedback, peer reviews]

Resources Provided: [e.g., access to tools, budget for training]

7. Team Member's Commitment

Ensure alignment and commitment from the team member.

Acknowledgement and Agreement:

I, [Team Member Name], am committed to following the development plan outlined above and actively participating in the process.

Signature: _____

Date: _____

8. Manager's Commitment

Reaffirm the manager's role in the process.

Acknowledgement and Agreement:

I, [Manager Name], commit to supporting [Team Member Name] in their development plan and providing guidance, resources, and feedback as needed.

Signature: _____

Date: _____

9. Review and Feedback

Document outcomes and feedback during the review process.

- **Progress Summary:**
  - Summarize achievements and areas for further improvement
- **Next Steps:**
  - Update goals, adjust plan as necessary

Review Date:

Signatures:

- **Team Member:** _____
- **Manager:** _____

This structured approach ensures clarity, alignment, and accountability, promoting a culture of continuous growth.

Pro Tip: *Encourage team members to dedicate 1–2 hours weekly for self-directed learning, whether through online courses, certifications, or reading industry blogs.*

Mentorship and Coaching for Career Growth

Mentorship and coaching play a vital role in professional growth, especially for junior team members looking to advance their careers. Think of mentorship as the big-picture guide and coaching as the day-to-day advice. A mentor might help a junior engineer map out their career path, while coaching focuses on immediate skills, such as debugging a tricky codebase or presenting a project update.

Creating a Mentorship Program:

1. **Pair Mentors and Mentees:** Match senior team members with junior ones based on goals, expertise, and compatibility.

2. **Define Goals and Expectations:** Set clear objectives for the mentorship, such as career guidance, skill-building, or networking.

3. **Regular Check-Ins:** Encourage mentors and mentees to meet regularly to discuss progress, challenges, and future steps.

4. **Evaluate Outcomes:** Periodically review the mentorship's impact, gathering feedback to improve the program.

Example: A senior network engineer mentors a junior engineer, helping them develop advanced network configuration and troubleshooting skills while offering career guidance.

Pro Tip: *Pair mentees with mentors outside their direct reporting line. This promotes fresh perspectives and minimizes potential biases.*

Mentorship Program Outline

A mentorship outline can help establish clear goals and expectations for the relationship.

Mentorship Focus	Mentor	Mentee	Meeting Frequency	Goals
Network Configuration Skills	Senior Network Engineer	Junior Network Engineer	Bi-weekly	Master specific configurations and protocols

- **Purpose:** Establish a structured mentorship program within the IT team, matching experienced professionals with newer team members to promote growth and knowledge-sharing.

- **Mentorship Program Framework** outlining the stages and objectives of the mentorship process.
  - Stages:
    - ➢ **Program Initiation**: Match mentors and mentees based on career goals and expertise.
    - ➢ **Goal Setting**: Define learning goals and expectations at the start.
    - ➢ **Regular Check-ins**: Schedule periodic meetings for guidance and feedback.
    - ➢ **Progress Review**: Midway review to assess growth and address any challenges.
    - ➢ **Conclusion**: Reflect on progress, review goals, and plan next steps.

Example Mentorship Program Outline Layout

Stage	Description	Frequency
Program Initiation	Match mentors and mentees	Beginning of program
Goal Setting	Set specific learning and development goals	Initial meeting
Regular Check-ins	Provide guidance and support	Biweekly or monthly
Progress Review	Evaluate growth and address challenges	Midway through program
Conclusion	Reflect on progress and set future development	End of program

Planning for Succession and Career Pathing

Succession planning ensures continuity by preparing team members to step into more senior roles as opportunities arise. Career pathing provides clear progression paths, boosting motivation and engagement by showing team members a future within the organization.

Steps for Career Pathing and Succession Planning:

1. **Identify Key Roles:** Determine critical roles within your team that would require a succession plan.

2. **Develop Progression Paths:** Outline potential career paths for each role, detailing the skills and experience needed to advance.

3. **Support Skill Development:** Provide training and development opportunities that prepare team members for higher-level roles.

4. **Review Regularly:** Revisit career plans periodically to ensure alignment with team members' goals and organizational needs.

Example: A succession plan for a data center manager might involve developing a lead technician's management and strategic planning skills to prepare them for future leadership.

Position	Next-Level Role	Required Skills/Experience	Development Plan
Junior Developer	Developer	Advanced programming skills, project experience	Take on complex projects
Developer	Senior Developer	Leadership in projects, proficiency in new tech	Leadership training
Senior Developer	Team Lead	Team management, strategic planning	Management course

Pro Tip: *Discuss career goals regularly during one-on-one meetings to ensure alignment between team members' aspirations and organizational opportunities.*

Closing Remarks

Professional development is a powerful tool for IT managers to strengthen team performance and drive innovation. By encouraging continuous learning, mentorship, and clear career paths, you enable your team to adapt and excel in a growing industry. This proactive investment leads to higher engagement, stronger retention, and a more dynamic IT environment.

As you prioritize your team's growth, you're not only enhancing individual skills but also building a strong and future-ready organization. The next chapter will explore how to apply strategic methodologies to further optimize IT management and operations.

CHAPTER 7
APPLYING AGILE, SCRUM, AND SIX SIGMA IN IT MANAGEMENT

Modern IT management thrives on Agile's flexibility, Scrum's structure, and Six Sigma's precision to address challenges and drive continuous improvement.

Introduction

Today's IT management often relies on the flexibility of Agile, the structured approach of Scrum, and the precision of Six Sigma. These methodologies can help you address challenges head-on and keep your team continuously improving. By combining the flexibility of Agile, the structured approach of Scrum, and the data-driven precision of Six Sigma, IT managers can deliver value more effectively. This chapter explores each framework, its applications in IT, and strategies for integration.

Overview of Agile, Scrum, and Six Sigma

Methodology	Focus Area	Key Benefits	Common Applications in IT
Agile	Iterative development and adaptability	Flexibility, faster time-to-market	Project management, DevOps
Scrum	Structured sprints for iterative delivery	Improved transparency, collaboration	Software development, sprint planning
Six Sigma	Process improvement through data analysis	Quality assurance, defect reduction	Incident management, process optimization

Agile:

Agile emphasizes iterative processes, collaboration, and adaptability to changing requirements.

- **Core Principles:**
  - Prioritize customer collaboration.
  - Deliver incremental improvements.
  - Adapt swiftly to changes.

Scrum:

Scrum, a subset of Agile, focuses on managing work in short cycles or "sprints."

- **Core Components:**
  - **Roles:** Product Owner, Scrum Master, Development Team.
  - **Artifacts:** Product Backlog, Sprint Backlog, Increment.
  - **Events:** Sprint Planning, Daily Stand-ups, Sprint Review, Retrospective.

Six Sigma:

Six Sigma is a data-driven methodology aimed at reducing defects and improving quality through disciplined problem-solving.

- **Core Phases (DMAIC):**
  - Define: Identify problems.
  - Measure: Quantify performance.
  - Analyze: Find root causes.
  - Improve: Implement solutions.
  - Control: Sustain improvements.

Comparing Agile, Scrum, and Six Sigma

Aspect	Agile	Scrum	Six Sigma
Scope	Flexible, adaptable methodology.	Framework within Agile for managing work cycles.	Data-driven approach for process improvement.
Focus	Adaptability to changes.	Transparency, collaboration, and incremental delivery.	Reducing defects and improving quality.

Key Metric	Customer satisfaction, velocity.	Sprint success rate, burndown charts.	Defect rate, process efficiency.
Team Structure	Cross-functional teams.	Defined roles (Scrum Master, Product Owner, Team).	Process analysts, quality improvement teams.
Primary Output	Working software or deliverables.	Incremental progress on prioritized goals.	Data-driven process enhancements.

Agile and Scrum in IT Management

Applications in IT:

1. **Project Management:** Agile enables IT managers to break large projects into manageable iterations, delivering value incrementally.

2. **DevOps:** Agile principles integrate with DevOps workflows to build teamwork and accelerate deployment cycles.

3. **Incident Management:** Agile processes allow teams to adapt quickly to address recurring IT issues.

Agile vs. Traditional Project Management in IT

Factor	Agile	Traditional
Planning	Iterative, flexible.	Fixed, upfront.
Delivery	Continuous, incremental.	At project completion.
Risk Management	Mitigated through iterative updates.	Identified upfront, harder to adjust.
Customer Involvement	High, throughout the process.	Limited to initial and final phases.

Scrum Roles in IT:

Role	Responsibility	Example in IT
Scrum Master	Facilitates Scrum events, removes blockers.	Ensures daily stand-ups focus on resolving impediments.
Product Owner	Manages the product backlog and priorities.	Prioritizes sprint goals for a software release.
Development Team	Completes work committed to during sprints.	Delivers an application module within a sprint cycle.

Pro Tip: *Use digital tools like Jira or Trello to visualize sprint progress. Clear visuals help the team stay aligned and identify bottlenecks quickly.*

Agile Adaptation for Small Teams

Agile methodologies can be tailored for teams with limited resources by focusing on essentials:

Agile Adaptation for Small Teams

The following flowchart illustrates how small IT teams can effectively adapt Agile practices to maximize efficiency while keeping workflows streamlined.

Step 1
Define priorities in a shared backlog

Step 2
Combine roles (e.g., Scrum Master and Product Owner)

Step 3
Use a Kanban board for simplified tracking

Step 4
Schedule weekly check-ins instead of full sprints

Step 5
Review and adapt goals monthly

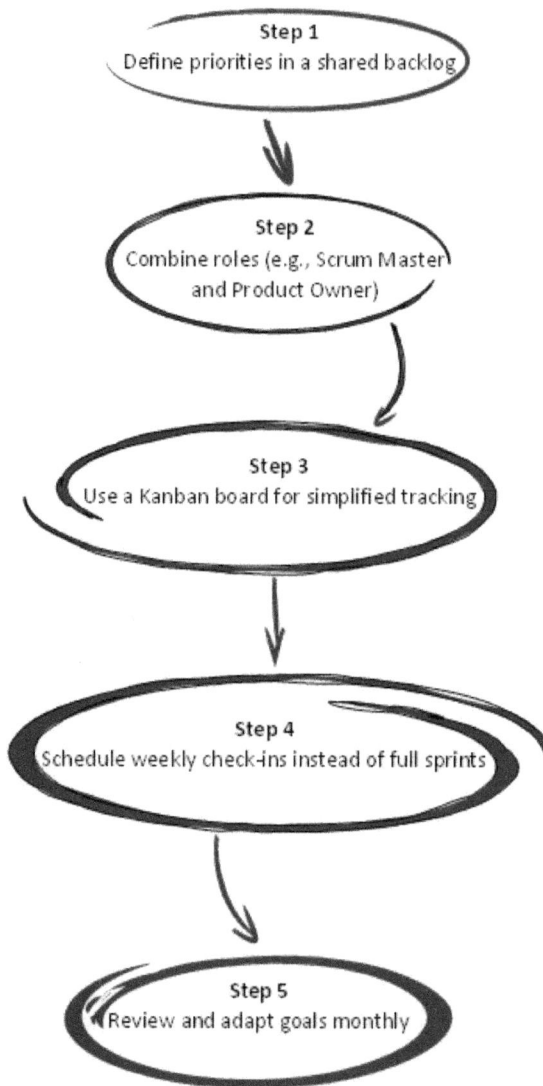

Pro Tip: *Keep workflows simple and adjust based on team feedback.*

Six Sigma in IT Management

Applications in IT:

1. **Service Delivery Optimization:** Minimize downtime and enhance service reliability.

2. **Incident Management:** Use root cause analysis to reduce recurring IT incidents.

3. **Quality Assurance:** Improve software reliability by identifying and addressing defects.

Common Six Sigma Tools in IT

Tool	Purpose	Example Usage in IT
Pareto Chart	Highlights the most significant issues.	Identifying common causes of system outages.
Fishbone Diagram	Identifies root causes of problems.	Analyzing recurring ticket delays.
Control Chart	Monitors process stability over time.	Ensuring consistent incident response times.

Pro Tip: *When using a Pareto chart, involve team members in identifying root causes of the most significant issues. Collaborative analysis improves both buy-in and solution quality.*

Case Study: Six Sigma for Incident Management

Scenario: A support team reduced ticket resolution times by using Six Sigma.

- Action Steps:
  - Used Pareto Analysis to identify key bottlenecks.

- Analyzed data to address common issues in ticket categorization.
- Streamlined the resolution process, reducing delays by 25%.

Integrating Agile, Scrum, and Six Sigma

Combining these methodologies provides IT managers with a robust framework for managing projects, improving processes, and delivering value.

Table: Integration Opportunities

Integration Aspect	Agile + Scrum Benefit	Six Sigma Contribution
Flexibility	Rapid adaptation to changing requirements.	Ensures process consistency.
Collaboration	Team-focused, promotes cross-functional teamwork.	Provides structured problem-solving.
Efficiency	Continuous improvement through iterative delivery.	Reduces waste and defects.

Example: Hybrid Approach for IT Operations

Scenario: An IT department used Scrum for task management and Six Sigma to improve ticket resolution times.

- Scrum provided clear workflows and daily coordination through stand-ups.
- Six Sigma tools analyzed incident data, identifying patterns that led to reduced delays.

Best Practices for IT Managers

1. **Adopt a Personalized Approach:** Customize Agile, Scrum, or Six Sigma methodologies to fit the IT environment's unique needs.

2. **Promote Collaboration:** Use Agile principles to encourage transparency and teamwork.

3. **Leverage Metrics:** Track key indicators like sprint velocity (Agile), resolution times (Scrum), and defect rates (Six Sigma).

4. **Integrate Automation:** Use tools like Jira for Agile and Scrum workflows, and Minitab for Six Sigma analysis.

Tools for Methodology Implementation

Methodology	Recommended Tools	Purpose
Agile	Jira, Trello	Sprint tracking, task management.
Scrum	Microsoft Azure DevOps, Monday.com	Backlog prioritization, sprint planning.
Six Sigma	Minitab, SigmaXL	Data analysis, process improvement.

Agile, Scrum, and Six Sigma provide IT managers with powerful methodologies to address operational challenges and drive continuous improvement. By leveraging Agile's adaptability, Scrum's structure, and Six Sigma's data-driven precision, IT managers can create a dynamic and efficient workflow that balances innovation with reliability. Success lies in understanding these methodologies' strengths and integrating them effectively into IT management practices.

Closing Remarks

Agile, Scrum, and Six Sigma provide powerful tools for IT managers to enhance team performance and streamline processes. By adopting the flexibility of Agile, the structure of Scrum, and the precision of Six Sigma, you can achieve continuous improvement and deliver high-value outcomes. As you integrate these methodologies into your workflows, the next chapter will guide you through navigating challenges and changes, including organizational shifts and crises.

CHAPTER 8
MANAGING ORGANIZATIONAL AND TECHNOLOGICAL CHANGES

Learn strategies for managing remote teams, handling organizational changes, and navigating crises effectively.

Handling Organizational and Technological Changes

Change is an inevitable part of IT, driven by the need for innovation, evolving business requirements, or organizational restructuring. Managing these changes effectively is crucial for maintaining productivity, morale, and team cohesion. This chapter will look deeper into strategies to handle both organizational and technological changes, emphasizing proactive communication, team involvement, and adaptive leadership.

Types of Changes in IT

1. **Technological Changes**

   - Deployment of new software, hardware upgrades, or cloud migration.

   - Example: Transitioning from on-premises data centers to cloud-based solutions.

2. **Organizational Changes**

   - Team restructuring, mergers, or leadership changes.

   - Example: Consolidating two IT departments post-merger to optimize resources.

3. **Process Changes**

   - Introducing new workflows, methodologies (e.g., Agile, DevOps), or compliance requirements.

   - Example: Shifting from a waterfall to an Agile project management framework.

Managing Small Teams and Nonprofit IT Operations

Small teams and nonprofit organizations face unique challenges, such as limited budgets, high staff turnover, and resource constraints. Here are strategies to succeed in such environments:

Budget-Conscious Motivation Techniques:

- **Public Recognition:** Highlight individual and team achievements during meetings.
- **Development Opportunities:** Provide access to free or low-cost online courses (e.g., Coursera, LinkedIn Learning).
- **Flexible Rewards:** Offer additional time off or cross-training as rewards.

Resource Allocation Best Practices:

- Prioritize tasks based on their impact on organizational goals.
- Use open-source tools to save on software costs.
- Leverage volunteers or interns for non-critical tasks.

Nonprofit-Specific Case Study:

A nonprofit IT department faced strict budget constraints while planning a cloud migration. To address this, they collaborated with a local university's computer science department to create an internship program, enabling student interns to assist with the migration. Under the supervision of the nonprofit's IT manager, the interns handled essential tasks, ensuring the project stayed on track without compromising quality.

This innovative partnership allowed the nonprofit to allocate limited resources to mission-focused priorities while successfully completing the migration. Simultaneously, it provided valuable real-world experience for aspiring IT professionals, highlighting the dual benefits of such collaborative efforts.

Change Management Strategies

To manage change effectively, IT managers should follow a structured approach, focusing on minimizing disruption and building a resilient team.

1. Communicate Clearly

- **Why it Matters:** Unclear communication breeds confusion and resistance. Providing clear and honest information helps build trust.
- **Best Practices:**
  - Announce changes as early as possible.
  - Use multiple channels (e.g., meetings, emails, dashboards) to reach all team members.
  - Share the rationale behind the change, expected benefits, and timelines.
  - Encourage questions to address concerns promptly.
- **Example:** During a major system overhaul, create a communication plan that includes weekly updates and a Q&A session.

2. Involve the Team

- **Why it Matters:** Inclusion promotes ownership and reduces resistance.

- **Best Practices:**
  - Involve team members in brainstorming solutions and planning implementation.
  - Assign roles that align with individual strengths and expertise.
  - Recognize contributions to encourage engagement.
- **Example:** When introducing a new incident management process, form a task force with representatives from different sub-teams to ensure diverse input.

3. Provide Training and Support

- **Why it Matters:** Equipping the team with the necessary skills minimizes anxiety and accelerates adaptation.
- **Best Practices:**
  - Offer hands-on training, workshops, or access to online resources.
  - Appoint a "change champion" or "super user" to provide peer support.
  - Set up a feedback loop to address training gaps.
- **Example:** When migrating to a cloud platform, organize a phased training program customized to different roles (e.g., developers, system admins).

4. Monitor and Adjust

- **Why it Matters:** Changes rarely go as planned; monitoring allows course correction.
- **Best Practices:**
  - Conduct regular check-ins to assess the impact of changes.

- Use metrics like productivity, error rates, or feedback scores to gauge success.
  - Be flexible—if something isn't working, adjust the plan.
- **Example:** After implementing a new ticketing system, track ticket resolution times and gather feedback from users and technicians.

Change Management Model

Stage	Action	Outcome
Awareness	Communicate the need and rationale for change.	Team understands the "why" of the change.
Desire	Highlight benefits and involve the team in decision-making.	Team is motivated to support the change.
Knowledge	Provide training and access to learning resources.	Team gains the skills needed.
Ability	Implement the change with hands-on guidance.	Team can successfully apply new methods.
Reinforcement	Follow up with feedback sessions and periodic reviews.	Sustained adoption and continuous improvement.

Justifying IT Investments to Senior Leadership

Convincing senior leadership to allocate resources for IT initiatives often requires more than technical know-how; it demands a clear alignment between the proposed project and the organization's strategic objectives. A strong, well-thought-out business case can connect the dots between technical possibilities and executive buy-in by clearly highlighting the tangible benefits in terms that matter to decision-makers.

Crafting a Business Case

1. **Focus on ROI (Return on Investment):** Senior leaders prioritize investments yield measurable returns. Highlight how the proposed IT initiative will contribute to cost savings, revenue growth, or operational efficiency. Quantify the benefits whenever possible to strengthen your argument.

   - *Example:* "Implementing an automated monitoring system will reduce downtime by 20%, saving $100,000 annually while improving system reliability and reducing customer complaints."

2. **Use Data to Support Claims:** Hard numbers, case studies, and benchmarks from similar projects in the industry can provide credibility to your proposal. Provide specific metrics and forecasts to support your claims and demonstrate thorough analysis.

   - *Example:* "A competitor who adopted a similar cloud-based CRM system experienced a 30% increase in sales team efficiency within the first year."

3. **Speak Their Language:** Avoid technical jargon and translate IT benefits into business outcomes. Frame the proposal in terms of what matters most to leadership, such as customer satisfaction, market competitiveness, or regulatory compliance. Use relatable analogies or simplified explanations when necessary to ensure clarity.

   - *Example:* "Enhancing our data security infrastructure will not only safeguard sensitive customer information but also protect the company's reputation, reducing the risk of costly breaches and potential legal liabilities."

4. **Align with Strategic Goals:** Demonstrate how the project supports broader organizational objectives. Whether it's

expanding into new markets, improving customer retention, or driving digital transformation, tie your proposal to the company's vision and priorities.

- *Example:* "Migrating to a scalable cloud platform aligns with our growth strategy by enabling faster time-to-market for new products and services."

5. **Provide a Risk Assessment:** Address potential risks and outline mitigation strategies. This shows leadership that you've considered challenges and have a proactive plan to handle them.

- *Example:* "While the initial migration may temporarily disrupt workflows, a phased implementation plan with comprehensive training sessions will minimize downtime and ensure a smooth transition."

6. **Include Visual Aids:** Use charts, graphs, and infographics to present complex data in a digestible format. A well-designed visual can make your case more compelling and memorable.

- *Example:* A bar chart showing projected cost savings over five years compared to the initial investment.

7. **Showcase Quick Wins:** Highlight early benefits or low-hanging fruits that can be achieved shortly after implementation. This demonstrates value and builds confidence in the project's success.

- *Example:* "In the first three months, automating manual reporting tasks will save 500 hours of employee time, allowing staff to focus on strategic initiatives."

Presenting a compelling case for IT investments requires a strategic approach that connects the dots between technical solutions and business outcomes. By focusing on ROI, leveraging data, and communicating in terms that resonate with senior leadership, you can significantly improve the likelihood of securing funding and support for your initiatives.

Addressing Common Challenges

1. Resistance to Change

- **Cause:** Fear of the unknown, lack of trust, or misaligned priorities.
- **Solution:**
    - Listen to concerns and validate emotions.
    - Address fears by emphasizing support and long-term benefits.
    - Share success stories from other teams or organizations.

2. Skill Gaps

- **Cause:** Rapid technological shifts leaving team members underprepared.
- **Solution:**
    - Conduct a skill assessment before implementing changes.
    - Invest in upskilling through certifications, courses, or mentorship.
    - Provide a "sandbox" environment for hands-on practice.

3. Inconsistent Leadership

- **Cause:** Mixed messages or lack of alignment among leaders.
- **Solution:**
    - Ensure all leaders are aligned on goals and messaging.
    - Hold leadership meetings to maintain consistency.
    - Empower middle managers to act as effective change agents.

Case Study: Adopting DevOps Practices

Scenario: An IT team was transitioning from traditional IT workflows to DevOps methodologies, aiming for faster delivery and better partnership between development and operations.

Actions Taken:

- **Communication Plan:** Leadership held a town hall to explain the goals and benefits of DevOps.
- **Team Involvement:** Cross-functional teams were formed to pilot DevOps practices in smaller projects.
- **Training Program:** Certifications and workshops were provided for CI/CD tools like Jenkins and Docker.
- **Feedback Loop:** Weekly retrospectives were held to gather input and refine processes.

Outcomes:

- 30% faster project delivery times within the first six months.
- Increased collaboration and reduced siloed workflows.
- Higher job satisfaction among team members due to skill development.

Performance Tracking: A Change Management Dashboard

Metric	Pre-Change Baseline	Target	Current	Notes
Employee Engagement Score	75%	85%	82%	Post-training surveys show improvement.
System Downtime	10 hours/month	5 hours/month	6 hours/month	Gradual improvement

				since new processes.
Change Adoption Rate	N/A	90%	88%	Need more follow-up training sessions.
Average Project Completion Time	8 weeks	6 weeks	7 weeks	Pilot projects showing faster turnarounds.

Professional Development Plan Post-Change

Team Member	Skill Gap Identified	Training Plan	Timeline	Success Criteria
John Smith	Limited knowledge of CI/CD tools	Jenkins Certification Course	3 months	Completes certification, applies tools in projects.
Jessica Clark	Leadership during transitions	Change Management Workshop	2 months	Leads a successful change initiative.
Andrew King	Cloud Platform Expertise	AWS Solutions Architect Pathway	6 months	Migrates 3 applications to AWS.

By following these strategies and leveraging tools like dashboards, training programs, and structured feedback mechanisms, IT managers can effectively navigate challenges and changes and set their teams up for long-term success.

Change Management Model Flow Chart

A change management model can guide teams through each stage of adaptation.

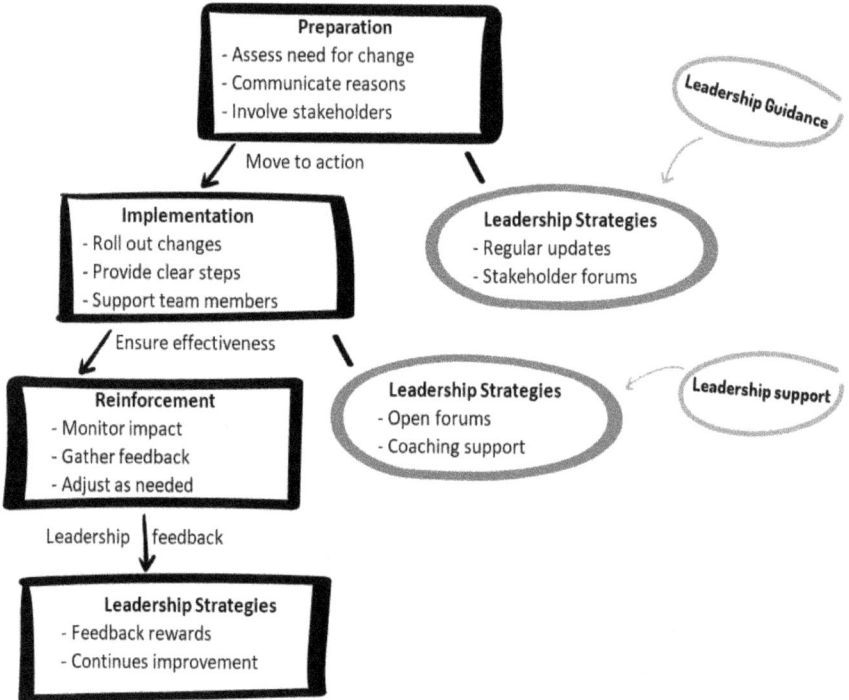

Service Level Agreements (SLA) and Operational Level Agreements (OLA)

Service-Level Agreements (SLAs) and Operational-Level Agreements (OLAs) are foundational to managing expectations, ensuring accountability, and delivering high-quality IT services. While SLAs focus on commitments between service providers and customers, OLAs define the internal agreements necessary to meet those commitments. This section explores their significance, structure, and best practices in IT management.

What Are SLA and OLA?

Service Level Agreement (SLA): An SLA is a formal agreement between an IT service provider and its customer that defines the expected level of service.

Key Components:

- Service scope (e.g., uptime, response times).
- Performance metrics (e.g., 99.9% availability).
- Penalties for non-compliance (e.g., credits, fee reductions).

Operational Level Agreement (OLA): An OLA is an internal agreement between IT teams or departments to ensure the SLA commitments are met.

Key Components:

- Responsibilities of internal teams.
- Performance targets that align with SLA goals.
- Processes for issue resolution and escalation.

Differences Between SLA and OLA

Aspect	SLA	OLA
Purpose	Agreement with customers	Internal agreement within the organization
Audience	External stakeholders (e.g., clients)	Internal stakeholders (e.g., IT teams)
Focus	Service delivery and accountability	Operational alignment and collaboration
Enforcement	Binding contract	Organizational policy

Example:

An SLA might guarantee a client 99.9% uptime for their cloud application, while an OLA ensures the internal infrastructure team monitors server performance every 15 minutes to meet this SLA.

Crafting Effective SLAs

Steps to Create an SLA:

1. **Define the Scope of Service:** Identify what is included and excluded from the agreement (e.g., services provided, supported platforms).
2. **Set Clear Metrics:** Use measurable indicators such as:
   - Uptime percentage (e.g., 99.9% availability).
   - Mean Time to Resolve (MTTR).
   - First Response Time.
3. **Agree on Penalties:** Outline repercussions for failing to meet service levels (e.g., financial **credits**).
4. **Include Reporting Mechanisms:** Detail how performance will be tracked and **reported** (e.g., monthly dashboards).
5. **Review Regularly:** Update **SLAs** periodically to reflect evolving customer needs or service capabilities.

Sample SLA Template:

Section	Details
Service Scope	Cloud hosting for client applications
Uptime Guarantee	99.9% availability
Response Time	Within 30 minutes for critical issues

Reporting Frequency	Monthly service reports
Penalties	5% service credit for non-compliance

Structuring OLAs

Steps to Create an OLA:

1. **Identify Interdependencies:** Map out which teams are involved in meeting the SLA goals (e.g., network, security, application support).

2. **Define Team Responsibilities:** Clearly specify each team's role in delivering services (e.g., server monitoring, incident response).

3. **Set Internal Metrics:** Establish performance metrics that align with SLA targets (e.g., internal resolution times, monitoring frequencies).

4. **Establish Escalation Paths:** Ensure a defined process for escalating issues to higher-level management or specialized teams.

Example OLA:

Section	Details
Service Team	Network Operations Center (NOC)
Monitoring Frequency	Every 15 minutes
Incident Response	Acknowledge within 5 minutes, resolve within 1 hour
Escalation	To Tier 2 support after 30 minutes of no resolution

Best Practices for SLA and OLA Management

1. **Alignment Between SLA and OLA:**
   - Ensure internal OLAs support the external SLAs.

- For instance, if the SLA guarantees a 1-hour resolution time, the OLA should specify internal response times that allow this.

2. **Regular Reviews:**
   - Conduct quarterly SLA/OLA reviews with stakeholders to identify areas for improvement.
   - Use performance data to refine metrics and update terms.

3. **Automated Monitoring:**
   - Implement tools like SolarWinds or ServiceNow to track SLA/OLA performance and generate real-time alerts for potential breaches.

4. **Stakeholder Involvement:**
   - Involve all relevant teams in SLA/OLA creation to ensure practical and achievable commitments.

SLA and OLA Workflow Example

Step	Action	Responsible Party
Incident Detection	Alert triggered by monitoring tool	Monitoring Team
Initial Response	Acknowledge the incident within 5 mins	Incident Response Team (OLA metric)
Resolution	Resolve issue within 1 hour	Application Support Team (OLA metric)
Reporting	Submit incident report within 24 hours	IT Manager (SLA metric)

Real-World Case Study: SLA/OLA Alignment

Scenario:

A managed service provider (MSP) promised clients 99.95% system availability in their SLA but faced challenges meeting this target due to internal inefficiencies.

Actions Taken:

1. Developed OLAs between the NOC and application support teams to improve response times.
2. Introduced real-time performance dashboards to track OLA compliance.
3. Trained teams on proactive monitoring techniques to address issues before they escalated.

Outcome:

The MSP achieved SLA compliance for six consecutive months, leading to higher customer satisfaction and contract renewals.

SLAs and OLAs are essential for ensuring accountability, consistency, and quality IT services. By aligning internal operations with external commitments, IT managers can build trust with customers and enhance teamwork within teams. Regular reviews, measurable metrics, and leveraging automated tools ensure these agreements remain effective in a constantly evolving IT environment.

Managing IT During Mergers and Acquisitions

Mergers and acquisitions (M&A) often present organizations with unique challenges, and IT integration is one of the most critical components for ensuring the success of such endeavors. Seamlessly integrating IT systems and processes can streamline operations, reduce redundancies, and align the merged entities with strategic goals.

Key Steps for Effective IT Integration:

1. **Inventory Assets:** Begin with a comprehensive audit of both organizations' IT infrastructures. This step involves cataloging hardware, software, licenses, and third-party services. Identifying redundancies, gaps, and incompatibilities early helps set the stage for smoother integration.

Example: A merger between two financial institutions revealed overlapping customer relationship management (CRM) tools. By identifying these redundancies during the inventory phase, the organizations avoided costly duplication and aligned their CRM strategy with customer-centric objectives.

2. **Align Strategies:** Ensure that IT goals align with the overarching vision of the merged entity. This involves not only technical alignment but also strategic planning. IT leaders must collaborate with key stakeholders to define clear priorities, such as which systems to retain, upgrade, or retire.

Example: During the acquisition of a smaller tech company, a multinational enterprise integrated the acquired firm's cloud-native solutions into its existing infrastructure. This strategic alignment enhanced scalability and supported the company's long-term innovation goals.

3. **Address Cultural Shifts:** Mergers bring together different organizational cultures, which can significantly impact IT teams. Facilitating open communication and providing cross-training opportunities help bridge cultural gaps and build a unified team

spirit. Change management strategies should address potential resistance and promote collaboration.

Example: In a recent merger, one organization integrated duplicate systems to simplify operations and improve efficiency. To ensure a smooth transition, cross-functional workshops were held, allowing IT teams from both companies to share expertise and adapt to the unified processes. This approach strengthened teamwork and ensured the successful implementation of the new systems.

4. **Assess Risks and Plan for Contingencies:** IT integration during M&A is filled with potential risks, such as data breaches, system downtimes, and compliance issues. Developing a robust risk management plan is crucial. This includes regular testing, backup strategies, and clear escalation protocols to handle unforeseen challenges.

5. **Monitor and Optimize Post-Integration:** IT integration doesn't end once systems are merged. Continuous monitoring ensures that the integrated infrastructure is performing as expected. Regular reviews and feedback loops can identify areas for further optimization, ensuring the IT systems continue to support the organization's evolving needs.

Effective IT integration is more than just a technical exercise, it's a strategic imperative that can greatly influence the success of mergers and acquisitions. By inventorying assets, aligning strategies, addressing cultural shifts, and proactively managing risks, organizations can unlock the full potential of their combined resources and position themselves for sustained growth in a competitive marketplace.

Closing Remarks

Organizational and technological changes need clear communication, team involvement, and flexible leadership. By handling transitions well and seeing challenges as chances to grow, you can build a strong team ready to man age the demands of IT operations. The next chapter will focus on disaster prevention and recovery, giving you practical ways to protect your IT environment.

CHAPTER 9
IT MANAGER'S ROLE IN DISASTER PREVENTION AND RECOVERY

As the primary architect of organizational resilience, the IT manager plays a critical role in preparing for, mitigating, and recovering from disasters.

Disasters—natural, technical, or human-made— can significantly disrupt IT operations, jeopardizing business continuity, data integrity, and customer trust. Disaster prevention and recovery are not merely technical concerns but strategic imperatives that require careful planning and management. The IT manager plays a pivotal role in orchestrating these efforts, balancing proactive measures with reactive strategies to ensure operational resilience. This chapter digs deeper into disaster prevention, recovery, and the critical role of the IT manager in safeguarding organizational assets.

The Scope of IT Disasters

Disasters in IT can take various forms, each requiring a tailored approach for prevention and recovery:

- **Natural Disasters:** Hurricanes, floods, earthquakes, or fires that damage physical infrastructure.
- **Technological Failures:** Server crashes, hardware malfunctions, or software bugs causing operational downtime.
- **Cybersecurity Threats:** Ransomware encrypting critical dataCoordinate incident response, and escalate to security teams.
- **Human Errors:** Misconfigurations, accidental data deletions, or policy violations.

Role of the IT Manager:

The IT manager identifies vulnerabilities, establishes response protocols, and coordinates disaster management efforts.

Common IT Disasters and Managerial Focus

Disaster Type	Example	IT Manager's Focus
Natural Disaster	Flood damaging a data center	Activate failover systems and ensure offsite backups.
Technological Failure	Server crash during peak hours	Oversee root cause analysis and initiate recovery protocols.
Cybersecurity Threat	Ransomware encrypting critical data	Coordinate incident response, escalate to security teams.
Human Error	Misconfigured firewall	Implement monitoring to catch and correct errors.

Disaster Prevention: The IT Manager's Strategic Role

Preventing disasters requires proactive planning and a structured approach.

Key Prevention Strategies:

1. **Risk Assessments:**
   - Regularly evaluate system vulnerabilities, cybersecurity risks, and process gaps.
   - Collaborate with internal stakeholders to address cross-departmental dependencies.

2. **Cybersecurity Integration:**
   - Implement firewalls, intrusion detection systems (IDS), and encryption protocols.
   - Enforce multi-factor authentication (MFA) and least-privilege access policies.

3. **Data Backup and Redundancy:**
   - Automate backups to geographically diverse locations.

- Regularly test backups to ensure data recoverability and integrity.

4. **System Monitoring:**
   - Deploy real-time monitoring tools to detect anomalies.
   - Use predictive analytics to address potential system failures before they occur.

IT Manager's Role in Prevention:

- **Policy Maker:** Develop disaster prevention policies and align them with industry standards.

- **Educator:** Establish training programs to build a security-first mindset among employees.

- **Budget Advocate:** Secure funding for preventive technologies like advanced firewalls or redundancy systems.

Disaster Recovery Planning (DRP): A Manager's Blueprint

An effective Disaster Recovery Plan (DRP) serves as the foundation for IT resilience.

Core Components of a DRP:

1. **Business Impact Analysis (BIA):**
   - Identify mission-critical systems and their dependencies.
   - Assess the financial and operational impacts of system downtime.

2. **Cybersecurity-Integrated Recovery Objectives:**
   - **Recovery Point Objective (RPO):** Define the maximum tolerable data loss.

- **Recovery Time Objective (RTO):** Set the maximum acceptable downtime.

3. **Documented Procedures:**
   - Create step-by-step recovery guides for all major IT systems.
   - Include escalation paths for incidents involving senior management.

4. **Testing and Maintenance:**
   - Schedule routine disaster recovery drills.
   - Update the DRP based on simulation results and emerging threats.

Pro Tip: *Test your disaster recovery plan quarterly with simulated scenarios. Regular testing uncovers gaps and ensures the team is prepared for actual incidents.*

IT Manager's Role in DRP Implementation:

- **Lead Planner:** Oversee DRP creation and ensure it aligns with organizational goals.
- **Drill Coordinator:** Conduct recovery simulations to test team readiness.
- **Escalation Point:** Notify senior management and provide actionable updates during critical incidents.

Disaster Recovery Templates

A structured approach to disaster recovery ensures clarity and speed during crises. Use these templates as starting points:

Step	Action	Owner
Risk Assessment	Identify potential risks.	IT Manager
Backup Verification	Test data backups.	Backup Specialist
Vendor Coordination	Confirm vendor SLAs.	Vendor Liaison
Post-Recovery Analysis	Document lessons learned.	Team Leads

Quick Recovery Toolkit:

- Tools: Backup software (e.g., Veeam), monitoring dashboards (e.g., Zabbix).

- Checklist: Verify power systems, restore network connectivity, and test applications.

Use these tools to ensure a faster recovery while minimizing downtime.

Sample Escalation Path for Cybersecurity Incidents

Incident Severity	IT Manager Action	Escalation Level
Low	Mitigate internally, log the incident.	No escalation required.
Medium	Notify department head, execute DRP.	Departmental leadership informed.
High	Activate response team, escalate to CIO/CTO.	Senior management and external stakeholders informed.

Cybersecurity as a Disaster Prevention Pillar

Cybersecurity is critical to disaster prevention and recovery, directly impacting the IT manager's role.

Key Cybersecurity Practices:

1. **Threat Intelligence:**
   - Stay informed about emerging threats through threat intelligence platforms.
   - Share threat insights with the team to preempt potential vulnerabilities.

2. **Incident Response Planning:**
   - Develop playbooks for common cybersecurity incidents (e.g., phishing, malware).
   - Include defined escalation paths and stakeholder communication plans.

3. **Continuous Compliance Monitoring:**
   - Ensure adherence to regulations like GDPR, HIPAA, or PCI DSS.
   - Conduct regular audits to identify gaps in compliance.

IT Manager's Role in Cybersecurity:

- **Incident Commander:** Lead the response to cybersecurity breaches and ensure proper escalation.
- **Communicator:** Keep senior leaders informed about potential risks and incident updates.
- **Strategist:** Integrate cybersecurity tools into the DRP for a comprehensive response strategy.

Pro Tip: *Conduct monthly phishing simulations to raise awareness and reinforce secure practices among team members.*

Post-Disaster Recovery: From Recovery to Improvement

Recovering from disasters isn't the end; it's an opportunity to strengthen systems and processes.

Steps for Post-Disaster Recovery:

1. **Restore Operations:**
   - Focus on restoring mission-critical systems first.
   - Leverage redundant backups for faster recovery.

2. **Analyze and Learn:**
   - Conduct a post-mortem analysis to identify the root cause of the disaster.
   - Document lessons learned and update the DRP accordingly.

3. **Communicate Outcomes:**
   - Provide detailed recovery updates to senior management and stakeholders.
   - Share recovery metrics (e.g., RTO/RPO compliance) to demonstrate resilience.

Disaster Prevention Framework

Phase	Activities	IT Manager's Role
Assessment	Risk evaluations and threat analysis.	Oversee cross-departmental assessments.
Mitigation	Backup, redundancy, and cybersecurity.	Allocate resources for preventive measures.
Monitoring	Real-time system and network monitoring.	Select and manage monitoring tools.
Training	Employee education on protocols.	Conduct awareness programs and mock drills.

IT Manager's Role in Post-Recovery:

- **Process Evaluator:** Identify gaps in the disaster response and recommend improvements.

- **Stakeholder Liaison:** Communicate outcomes and lessons learned to senior leadership.

- **Continuous Improver:** Update policies, tools, and training based on post-disaster insights.

Pro Tip: *Document key learnings and action steps in a centralized knowledge base for easy reference during future incidents.*

Recovery Metrics Dashboard

Metric	Target	Current Status	IT Manager Action
RPO Compliance	Data loss < 15 minutes	20 minutes (needs improvement)	Investigate backup scheduling gaps.
RTO Compliance	Downtime < 2 hours	1.5 hours (on track)	Continue to monitor recovery workflows.
Incident Escalation Time	<30 minutes	45 minutes (needs improvement)	Optimize escalation paths and training.

Closing Remarks

Disaster prevention and recovery are critical for maintaining operational continuity in IT environments. You can minimize risks and ensure swift recovery by implementing robust disaster recovery plans, investing in cybersecurity, and learning from post-incident reviews. The next chapter will address financial management, offering insights into optimizing IT budgets and resource allocation.

CHAPTER 10
FINANCIAL MANAGEMENT IN IT OPERATIONS

Effective financial management is key to aligning IT initiatives with business goals, covering budgeting, expense management, and balancing CapEx and OpEx.

Effective financial management is a cornerstone of successful IT management. From planning budgets and managing expenses to working with vendors and balancing CapEx (Capital Expenditures) and OpEx (Operational Expenditures), IT managers need a clear understanding of financial principles to align technology initiatives with business goals. This chapter explores these critical aspects and provides practical strategies for IT managers.

Budgeting for IT Operations

Budgeting is essential for ensuring IT teams have the necessary resources while staying aligned with organizational goals.

Steps to Develop an IT Budget:

1. **Assess Current Needs:** Analyze existing expenses, including recurring costs such as software subscriptions and licenses, hardware upgrades, and operational costs.

2. **Forecast Future Requirements:** Predict costs for upcoming projects upcoming projects, such as migrations, upgrades, or new implementations. Incorporate emerging technologies that may require investment, like enhanced cybersecurity measures.

3. **Categorize Expenses:** Divide expenses into fixed costs (e.g., cloud subscriptions) and variable costs (e.g., project-based expenses).

4. **Engage Stakeholders:** Collaborate with department heads to align the IT budget with organizational priorities.

5. **Monitor and Adjust:** Conduct monthly or quarterly budget reviews to track spending and adapt to changing conditions, such as unexpected vendor price increases or surging cloud usage costs.

Example Budget Allocation Table:

Expense Category	Estimated Cost	Percentage of Total Budget
Infrastructure	$500,000	40%
Software Licenses	$300,000	24%
Staffing & Training	$200,000	16%
Security	$150,000	12%
Miscellaneous	$100,000	8%

Pro Tip: *Categorize expenses into "must-haves" and "nice-to-haves" to ensure essential investments are prioritized during budget cuts.*

Affordable Tools for Monitoring and Security

For IT teams with budget constraints, consider these affordable or open-source options:

1. **Monitoring:**

   - **PRTG Network Monitor:** Ideal for small setups, offering a free version for up to 100 sensors.

   - **LibreNMS:** A community-driven network monitoring platform that is scalable and customizable.

2. **Security:**

   - **ClamAV:** An open-source antivirus solution that is effective for basic malware detection.

   - **Wazuh:** Open-source security platform offering SIEM (Security Information and Event Management) capabilities.

Managing Invoices and Vendor Relationships

Invoice Management

Invoices are critical for maintaining transparency and accountability in IT spending. IT managers should:

- **Verify Accuracy:** Cross-check invoices against vendor contracts and purchase orders.
- **Establish Payment Schedules:** Avoid late fees by adhering to agreed payment terms.
- **Track Spending:** Use financial software to track and categorize expenses for better oversight.

Vendor Management

Vendors, from hardware suppliers to cloud service providers, play a significant role in IT operations. Effective vendor management ensures reliability and cost efficiency.

Pro Tip: *Negotiate multi-year contracts with vendors to secure better pricing and reduce annual budget fluctuations.*

Best Practices for Vendor Management

1. **Evaluate Vendors Thoroughly:** Assess vendors based on cost, quality of service, and alignment with organizational needs.
2. **Maintain Clear Contracts:** Define deliverables, payment terms, and SLAs (Service Level Agreements) upfront.
3. **Build Strong Relationships:** Establish regular check-ins to address issues and encourage teamwork.
4. **Monitor Performance:** Use KPIs like uptime, response times, and resolution times to evaluate vendor performance.

Case Study: Vendor Consolidation

An IT department reduced operational costs by consolidating multiple software vendors into a single provider offering bundled solutions. The streamlined approach improved vendor communication and resulted in a 20% cost saving.

Understanding CapEx and OpEx in IT

Capital Expenditures (CapEx): CapEx refers to long-term investments in assets, such as servers, networking hardware, or data centers.

- **Characteristics:**
    - High upfront costs.
    - Depreciates over time.

    Examples: Buying a server, constructing a data center.

Operational Expenditures (OpEx): OpEx refers to ongoing expenses for maintaining daily operations, such as cloud subscriptions or managed services.

- **Characteristics:**
    - Paid regularly (e.g., monthly or annually).
    - Directly deductible as business expenses.

    Examples: Cloud hosting, software licenses.

CapEx vs. OpEx Comparison:

Aspect	CapEx	OpEx
Payment	One-time, large investment	Recurring, smaller payments
Flexibility	Low (requires approval cycles)	High (easier to adjust usage)

Tax Impact	Depreciated over several years	Fully deductible in the same year
Example	Purchasing physical servers	Cloud-based Infrastructure as a Service (IaaS)

Key Considerations:

- Use CapEx for predictable, long-term infrastructure needs.
- Opt for OpEx when scalability and flexibility are priorities, such as cloud computing.

Strategies for Balancing CapEx and OpEx

1. **Hybrid Approaches:** Combine CapEx (e.g., owned data centers) with OpEx (e.g., cloud services) to create a balanced IT infrastructure.

2. **Cost Analysis:** Regularly analyze the total cost of ownership (TCO) for both CapEx and OpEx investments.

3. **Align with Business Strategy:** Consider the organization's financial strategy. Some businesses prefer high CapEx for tax benefits, while others prioritize OpEx for flexibility.

Example: Transitioning to a Cloud-First Strategy

A company shifted its disaster recovery solutions from CapEx (on-premises servers) to OpEx (cloud backups). This move reduced upfront costs and allowed better scalability during peak seasons.

Tools for Financial Management in IT

- **IT Financial Management Tools:** Tools like Planview or CloudHealth help track, analyze, and optimize IT spending.

- **Invoice Management Software:** Platforms like SAP Ariba streamline invoice approvals and vendor payments.

- **Expense Reporting Tools:** Tools like Expensify provide real-time insights into expenditure trends.

- **Automation Solutions:** Tools like **Zapier** or **HubSpot** to automate invoice processing and approval workflows.

By carefully balancing budgeting, leveraging affordable tools, and mastering CapEx/OpEx dynamics, IT managers can create a financially sustainable roadmap for growth. Financial management in IT isn't just about controlling costs; it's about enabling innovation, ensuring operational efficiency, and aligning with business goals.

Sample Metrics for IT Management Success

Metric	Definition	Why It's Important
Budget Adherence (%)	Percentage of projects delivered within budget	Keeps finances under control
Incident Response Time	Average time to address IT incidents	Reduces downtime and improves service levels
Employee Turnover Rate	Percentage of team leaving annually	Signals team satisfaction and retention levels
Training Completion Rate	Percentage of planned training completed	Tracks skill-building progress

Closing Remarks:

Effective financial management is essential for running cost-efficient IT operations. You can align IT investments with organizational priorities by mastering budgeting, vendor management, and tracking operational expenses. The final chapter will discuss future trends and innovations, preparing you to lead your team into the next phase of IT management.

CHAPTER 11

FUTURE TRENDS AND INNOVATIONS IN IT MANAGEMENT

Prepare for the future by exploring emerging trends and innovations in IT management.

The IT industry is constantly evolving, shaped by emerging technologies, changing user demands, and a growing weight on security and sustainability. As an IT manager, staying informed and preparing your team for these shifts is essential. Success lies in anticipating change, equipping your team with the right skills, and integrating cutting-edge innovations into workflows.

This chapter dives into the key trends transforming IT management, provides tools to assess their impacts, and offers actionable strategies for preparing your team to adapt seamlessly.

Exploring Emerging Trends in IT Team Management

Emerging technologies and changing workforce dynamics present challenges and opportunities for IT managers. Understanding these trends enables proactive decisions, strategic investments in relevant skills, and smoother implementation of new tools.

Overview of Key Trends

1. **Artificial Intelligence (AI) and Machine Learning (ML):**

   - **Impact on IT:** AI and ML are increasingly used for tasks like data analysis, anomaly detection, and system optimization. They automate repetitive work, identify patterns, and enhance decision-making.

   - **Adaptation:** Train team members in AI and ML basics, invest in AI-driven tools, and encourage experimentation with predictive analytics solutions.

2. **Cybersecurity Enhancements:**

- **Impact on IT:** The shift to remote work and cloud-based solutions has amplified the need for advanced security protocols to counter sophisticated cyber threats.

- **Adaptation:** Provide ongoing security training, invest in AI-powered security tools, and establish robust incident response strategies.

3. **Cloud and Hybrid Computing:**

- **Impact on IT:** The rise of hybrid and multi-cloud environments demands new expertise in managing data and applications across platforms.

- **Adaptation:** Provide cloud certifications, implement hybrid-friendly tools, and optimize data management strategies.

4. **Data Privacy Regulations:**

- **Impact on IT:** Stringent privacy laws such as GDPR and CCPA mandate compliance-first approaches, with heavy penalties for non-compliance.

- **Adaptation:** Train staff on regulatory requirements, deploy tools to monitor compliance and conduct regular audits.

5. **Automation and Robotic Process Automation (RPA):**

- **Impact on IT:** RPA enables IT teams to streamline workflows and reduce manual effort, freeing resources for strategic projects.

- **Adaptation:** Familiarize the team with automation platforms and integrate RPA into everyday operations.

Trend Impact Matrix

By implementing a **Trend Impact Matrix** helps evaluating the influence of these trends on your team, allowing you to prioritize actions and allocate resources efficiently.

Trend	Impact Level	Projected Timeline	Team Impact
AI in IT Operations	High	Immediate to 2 years	Requires upskilling in AI tools and data analytics.
Cybersecurity Enhancements	High	Ongoing	Demands continuous training in security protocols.
Cloud & Hybrid Environments	Medium	Immediate to 5 years	Necessitates cloud certifications and hybrid architecture skills.
Data Privacy Regulations	High	Ongoing	Emphasizes compliance training and robust policy enforcement.
RPA & Automation	Medium	1-3 years	Encourages familiarity with automation platforms.

Preparing for Future Skills

Staying competitive in IT means being adaptable and constantly developing your expertise. As an IT Manager, you'll need to design and regularly update a **Future Skills Roadmap** that outlines the essential skills your team will require in the coming years.

Skills in Demand:

1. **AI and Data Analytics:** Understanding machine learning models and interpreting large datasets will be critical.

2. **Cloud Management:** Expertise in hybrid IT systems and multi-cloud platforms.

3. **Cybersecurity and Privacy:** Proficiency in threat detection and regulatory compliance.

4. **DevOps and Agile Practices:** Mastery of continuous delivery and collaboration tools.

5. **Automation Proficiency:** Familiarity with RPA and scripting to streamline processes.

Year	Skill	Focus Area	Training Resources
2024	Automation Proficiency	RPA tools, workflow automation	Vendor-specific training programs, online courses
2025	Advanced Cybersecurity	Threat detection, incident response	Certifications (CISSP, CEH, CompTIA Security+)
2026	Cloud Management	Hybrid architectures, containerization	AWS, Azure , and Google Cloud certifications
2027	AI and Data Analytics	Machine learning, data visualization	AI-focused bootcamps, certifications

Pro Tip: *To stay competitive, dedicate a portion of your team's time each quarter to exploring cutting-edge technologies, like AI or blockchain.*

Technological Forecasting Techniques

Forecasting helps IT managers anticipate changes and plan for technology adoption. Use these techniques to stay ahead of the curve:

1. **Horizon Scanning:** Systematically identify trends and potential disruptions

   Application: Review industry reports, attend tech conferences, and monitor tech publications.

2. **Scenario Planning:** Anticipate best- and worst-case outcomes of trends.

   Application: Prepare for disruptions in areas like cybersecurity or data privacy.

3. **Technology Roadmaps:** Strategically plan the adoption of new technologies.

   Application: Align team goals with future tech needs.

Adopting New Technologies

Adopting new technologies can face resistance if not managed effectively. A structured approach ensures smooth integration.

Best Practices Checklist

Action	Completed (✓)	Notes
Start with a pilot project	[✓]	Identify a small-scale application.
Gather team feedback	[✓]	Use surveys or one-on-one discussions.
Provide training resources	[✓]	Include tutorials, workshops, and Q&A sessions.
Track adoption rates	[✓]	Monitor weekly usage and report issues.

Preparing for Future Remote Work Innovations

The shift to remote and hybrid work models has transformed collaboration and security.

Key Innovations in Remote Work:

1. **Collaborative Tools:** Virtual whiteboards, real-time editing platforms, and messaging systems improve communication.

2. **Security Enhancements:** Biometric authentication and secure VPN alternatives enhance data protection.

3. **Performance Tracking:** Productivity dashboards promote autonomy and accountability.

Category	Examples	Benefits	Considerations
Collaborative Tools	Virtual whiteboards	Enhanced real-time collaboration	Ensure ease of use and integration.
Security Enhancements	Biometric authentication	Improved security for remote access	Compliance with privacy laws.
Performance Monitoring	Productivity dashboards	Encourages autonomy and accountability	Avoid over-surveillance concerns.

Future-Proofing IT Infrastructure

To stay ahead of rapid technological changes, adopt proactive strategies that ensure long-term stability and scalability.

Steps to Future-Proof IT Systems

1. **Adopt Cloud Solutions:** Shift to hybrid cloud architectures for flexibility.

- Example: Use AWS for scaling web applications during peak traffic.

2. **Regularly Evaluate Emerging Tech**: Schedule quarterly reviews of trends like AI, IoT, and edge computing to assess their relevance.

3. **Maintain Modular Architecture**: Design systems with interchangeable components to accommodate upgrades without overhauls.

Promoting Innovation Through an Experimentation Fund

Establishing an innovation fund empowers teams to explore new technologies.

Project	Funding Amount	Duration	Review Date	Expected Outcome
AI-driven monitoring pilot	$5,000	6 months	Quarterly review	Enhanced system efficiency
Remote access security	$3,000	3 months	End of project	Improved remote security protocols
Collaboration tool upgrade	$4,000	4 months	Bi-monthly check-in	Increased team productivity and satisfaction

In Summary

1. Emerging trends like AI, automation, and cybersecurity are reshaping IT management.

2. Use tools like the Trend Impact Matrix and Skills Roadmap to plan for the future.

3. Employ technological forecasting techniques to adapt proactively.

4. Encourage continuous learning and innovation through strategic investments.

By anticipating future challenges and trends, IT managers can lead strong, innovative teams that thrive in an ever-changing technological landscape.

Closing Remarks

As the IT landscape evolves, staying ahead of emerging trends and innovations is key to positioning your team for success. By anticipating future skill requirements, adopting new technologies, and adapting to the shift toward remote work, you can confidently guide your team into the future. The final chapter will summarize the key takeaways and offer practical advice for applying these insights effectively.

CHAPTER 12
RECAP OF KEY TAKEAWAYS

Effective IT team leadership blends technical expertise, strategic planning, and a people-first approach, emphasizing teamwork, adaptability, and a commitment to growth.

Managing an IT team effectively involves a combination of technical knowledge, leadership skills, and strategic planning. Throughout this book, we've covered essential aspects of IT team management, from setting up a solid foundation and choosing the right leadership style to promoting collaboration, handling conflict, managing performance, and preparing for future challenges.

Here's a summary of the core principles covered:

1. **Foundation and Team Dynamics**: Build a strong, cohesive team by understanding team dynamics, selecting the right people, and establishing clear roles.

2. **Leadership Styles and Adaptation:** Adjust your leadership approach to meet your team's needs and the demands of each project, all while shaping your own unique leadership philosophy.

3. **Communication and Collaboration:** Promote open dialogue and encourage teamwork to create a supportive, efficient team environment.

4. **Conflict Resolution and Problem-Solving:** Address conflicts proactively and instill a problem-solving culture.

5. **Performance Management and Motivation:** Set clear goals, conduct effective performance reviews, and motivate your team through recognition and development.

6. **Professional Development:** Invest in learning opportunities, mentorship, and career pathing to retain and grow top talent.

7. **Navigating Change:** Embrace organizational and technological changes with a structured approach to minimize disruption.

8. **Future-Readiness:** Equip your team with the skills to adapt to emerging trends and future challenges.

Table of Key Leadership Practices

This table can be a reference for managers to review core practices.

Key Area	Core Practice
Team Dynamics	Understand team roles and dynamics
Leadership Styles	Adapt based on project and team needs
Communication	Encourage open dialogue and feedback
Conflict Resolution	Address proactively and constructively
Performance Management	Set goals, review regularly, motivate
Professional Development	Provide training, mentorship, career paths
Change Management	Communicate, support, and reinforce
Future-Readiness	Develop skills for future challenges

Closing Remarks and Encouragement for Leaders

Leading an IT team is a dynamic, challenging, and rewarding experience. As a manager, you are in a unique position to drive projects, refine processes, and encourage your team members' professional growth and job satisfaction. Approach IT management with a mindset that values continuous learning, flexibility, and genuine empathy.

Remember, the most effective managers prioritize both the technical and human elements of leadership. Building trust, encouraging growth, and promoting a positive work environment will empower your team to reach new heights and contribute meaningfully to your organization's success.

Checklist for Ongoing Improvement

A final checklist provides managers with actionable steps to maintain growth and improvement.

Task	Frequency
Review team goals and alignment	Quarterly
Conduct one-on-one meetings	Weekly/Biweekly
Revisit personal leadership style	Annually
Organize team-building activities	Quarterly
Provide training and development	Biannually
Assess team readiness for new trends	Annually

Pro Tip: *Create a team-wide "learning day" once a quarter where members explore new technologies, methodologies, or certifications and share their findings.*

Final Thoughts

Managing an IT team in today's dynamic environment is both a challenge and an opportunity. As you implement the strategies outlined in this book, remember that leadership is a journey of continuous learning and adaptation. The tools and frameworks discussed here are not just for solving immediate problems but for laying the groundwork for a culture of innovation, resilience, and collaboration.

Let this book serve as a guide, but your growth as a leader will come from engaging with your team, listening to their ideas, and empowering them to reach their potential. The future of IT depends on leaders who can blend technical expertise with emotional intelligence and strategic vision. Step forward with confidence, lead with purpose, and create a legacy of excellence for your team.

APPENDIXES

The appendices provide hands-on tools, templates, and case studies to help you implement the strategies discussed throughout this book. These resources are designed to be practical and adaptable, allowing you to tailor them to the unique needs of your team. Think of them as your IT manager's toolkit; a quick reference to guide you through challenges and opportunities alike.

Appendix-A: Case Studies and Practical Examples for IT Managers

IT managers often face unique challenges that require a balance of strategic thinking, technical expertise, and strong leadership skills. This section provides real-world case studies and practical examples to help bridge the gap between theory and practice, illustrating how IT managers can address common issues and drive impactful results.

Each case study highlights a scenario where the role of the IT manager was essential in achieving success, whether it involved managing critical incidents, implementing new methodologies, improving team dynamics, or ensuring compliance with industry regulations. These examples are designed to provide actionable insights and strategies that you can adapt to your challenges. As you explore these scenarios, reflect on how similar strategies might apply to your experiences and challenges.

Case Study 1: Managing a Critical System Outage

Scenario:

A financial services company experienced a major server outage during peak hours, disrupting operations and causing potential revenue loss.

IT Manager's Role:

- **Leadership During Crisis:** The IT manager assembled the incident response team immediately.
- **Prioritization:** Delegated tasks such as identifying the root cause and isolating the issue.
- **Stakeholder Communication:** Provided regular updates to executives and business units about progress and expected resolution time.

Outcome:

The downtime was limited to 45 minutes, and the IT manager implemented new monitoring tools to prevent similar incidents, earning praise for clear communication and effective crisis management.

Case Study 2: Transitioning to Agile

Scenario:

An IT department consistently missed deadlines due to inflexible project management methodologies.

IT Manager's Role:

- **Driving Change:** Led the transition to Agile by organizing training sessions for team members.
- **Pilot Implementation:** Selected a smaller project to trial Agile practices, allowing the team to adapt incrementally.
- **Monitoring Progress:** Regularly reviewed team feedback and adjusted workflows to address challenges.

Outcome:

Project timelines improved by 35%, and the IT manager was recognized for promoting a collaborative environment and empowering the team to embrace a new methodology.

Case Study 3: Implementing a BYOD Policy

Scenario:

The company wanted to allow employees to use personal devices for work but had concerns about security risks.

IT Manager's Role:

- **Policy Development:** Drafted a BYOD policy outlining acceptable use, security requirements, and device management.
- **Tool Selection:** Evaluated and deployed a Mobile Device Management (MDM) solution to ensure compliance.
- **Employee Engagement:** Conducted workshops to train employees on secure practices and address concerns.

Outcome:

The IT manager's efforts improved productivity while maintaining security, with a 30% reduction in security incidents tied to personal device usage.

Case Study 4: Enhancing Data Security

Scenario:

A phishing attack exposed customer data, putting the company at risk of regulatory penalties.

IT Manager's Role:

- **Immediate Response:** The security team was directed to contain the breach and notified affected parties.
- **Long-Term Strategy:** Launched company-wide cybersecurity training and implemented stricter email filtering protocols.
- **Executive Reporting:** Presented a detailed post-incident analysis and proposed future safeguards to leadership.

Outcome:

The IT manager regained executive trust by transparently addressing the incident and reducing phishing vulnerabilities by 80%.

Case Study 5: Scaling Infrastructure for Growth

Scenario:

An e-commerce platform's infrastructure struggled to handle increased traffic during a promotional event.

IT Manager's Role:

- **Strategic Assessment:** Evaluated current system limitations and identified bottlenecks.
- **Cloud Migration Leadership:** Led the migration to a cloud-based solution with auto-scaling capabilities.
- **Team Coordination:** Ensured developers and operations staff collaborated effectively during the migration.

Outcome:

The IT manager successfully improved scalability, enabling the platform to handle 3x the traffic, and secured a 25% increase in sales during the next promotional event.

Case Study 6: Improving Employee Retention

Scenario:

High turnover in the IT team led to project delays and decreased morale.

IT Manager's Role:

- **Career Path Development:** Created a framework with clear progression opportunities for IT roles.
- **Mentorship Programs:** Paired senior staff with junior employees to encourage growth and knowledge sharing.

- **Recognition and Rewards:** Established a system to celebrate team accomplishments.

Outcome:

Retention rates improved by 40%, and the IT manager built a more motivated and engaged team, reducing recruitment costs.

Case Study 7: Reducing Incident Resolution Time

Scenario:

The IT help desk faced criticism for slow response times to critical issues.

IT Manager's Role:

- **Process Optimization:** Reorganized ticket prioritization based on urgency and impact.
- **Technology Integration:** Deployed automation to handle routine queries, freeing up technicians for complex issues.
- **Performance Tracking:** Established metrics to measure resolution times and held weekly reviews to ensure progress.

Outcome:

The average resolution time dropped from 6 hours to 2 hours, and customer satisfaction improved noticeably, highlighting operational success., earning praise from the IT manager for operational improvements.

Case Study 8: Migrating to a Hybrid Cloud

Scenario:

The company needed to reduce on-premises costs without compromising the security of critical workloads.

IT Manager's Role:

- **Cloud Strategy Development:** Assessed which workloads were suitable for public cloud migration.

- **Tool Implementation:** Deployed hybrid cloud management software to monitor and secure resources.

- **Team Upskilling:** Organized cloud certifications and training for team members.

Outcome:

Infrastructure costs dropped by 20%, and application uptime improved by 15%, highlighting the IT manager's ability to balance cost-efficiency with operational effectiveness.

Case Study 9: Managing a Cross-Functional Team

Scenario:

A major IT project required close collaboration between developers, network engineers, and security teams.

IT Manager's Role:

- **Facilitating Communication:** Set up regular cross-functional meetings to align objectives and ensure transparency.

- **Conflict Resolution:** Mediated disputes over resource allocation by emphasizing shared project goals.

- **Project Oversight:** Monitored progress and ensured adherence to the timeline.

Outcome:

The project was completed on time and under budget, and the IT manager was praised for promoting collaboration across departments.

Case Study 10: Preparing for a Data Privacy Audit

Scenario:

A healthcare company faced an upcoming GDPR compliance audit and identified process gaps.

IT Manager's Role:

- **Gap Analysis:** Conducted a thorough review of data storage and handling practices.
- **Policy Implementation:** Introduced data encryption and updated access controls.
- **Audit Readiness Training:** Educated staff on GDPR principles and their roles in compliance.

Outcome:

The company passed the audit without penalties, and the IT manager established ongoing compliance reviews to maintain readiness for future audits.

Case Study 11: Implementing AI-Driven Predictive Maintenance in a Data Center

Scenario:

A global enterprise planned to migrate its primary data center to a new location to improve infrastructure reliability. The challenge was to ensure minimal downtime and uninterrupted availability of critical applications during the migration.

IT Manager's Role:

- **Comprehensive Planning:** Developed a phased migration strategy, prioritizing critical systems for the initial move.

- **Risk Assessment:** Identified potential risks, including data loss and extended downtime, and implemented mitigation plans, such as redundant backups and failover systems.

- **Team Coordination:** Assembled cross-functional teams, including network engineers, database administrators, and application specialists, to manage the migration.

- **Stakeholder Communication:** Provided regular updates to executives and end-users, setting clear expectations about the migration timeline and potential disruptions.

Outcome:

The IT manager achieved a seamless migration with only 15 minutes of planned downtime for non-critical systems. Post-migration performance improved by 20%, and the new facility offered enhanced scalability and disaster recovery capabilities, positioning the organization for future growth.

Case Study 12: Implementing Disaster Recovery for a Multi-Region Data Center

Scenario:

A multinational corporation requires a robust disaster recovery (DR) solution to ensure business continuity across multiple regional data centers prone to natural disasters.

IT Manager's Role:

- **Risk Analysis:** Assessed the risk factors for each data center, such as earthquakes, floods, and power outages, and determined the likelihood and impact of various disasters.

- **Solution Design:**
    - Implemented an active-active architecture where workloads could instantly failover between regional data centers.
    - Leveraged software-defined networking (SDN) to enable dynamic traffic rerouting during outages.
    - **Replication Strategy:** Used synchronous replication for critical data and asynchronous replication for less time-sensitive information to balance speed and cost.

- **Testing and Validation:**
    - Conducted bi-annual disaster recovery drills to test failover mechanisms and identify weaknesses in the DR plan.
    - Trained staff to handle failovers effectively, ensuring minimal downtime during real events.

- **Stakeholder Communication:** Created dashboards for executives to monitor DR readiness and recovery time objectives (RTOs).

Outcome:

The IT manager's disaster recovery solution ensured near-zero downtime during a severe regional power outage, protecting critical operations and saving the company millions in potential losses.

Case Study 13: Consolidating IT Post-Merger

Scenario: A financial services firm merged with a tech startup, creating redundant CRM systems.

IT Manager's Role:

- Conducted a joint audit to inventory software and licenses.
- Consolidated CRM into Salesforce, migrating historical data.
- Provided cross-training on unified systems to both teams.

Outcome:

- Reduced annual CRM costs by 30%.
- Improved customer service ratings due to streamlined operations.

Case Study 14: Achieving HIPAA Compliance

Scenario:

A healthcare provider needs to comply with HIPAA for patient data storage.

IT Manager's Role:

- Conducted an internal compliance audit using Nessus.
- Implemented **Microsoft Azure** for encrypted data storage with access controls, leveraging services like **Azure Storage** (with encryption at rest), **Azure Active Directory (AAD)** for role-based access, and **Azure Key Vault** for managing encryption keys.
- Trained staff on handling protected health information.

Outcome:

- Passed HIPAA audit with zero critical findings.
- Improved patient trust and reduced liability risks.

Case Study 15: Automating Routine IT Tasks

Scenario:

An IT department struggled with repetitive tasks such as account provisioning, password resets, and system monitoring, leading to wasted time and high costs.

IT Manager's Role:

- **Assessment:** Identified tasks suitable for automation using RPA (Robotic Process Automation) tools.
- **Implementation:** Introduced an automation framework to streamline account provisioning and monitoring.
- **Training:** Provided workshops for staff to upskill in automation tools and monitoring frameworks.

Outcome:

The team was able to focus more on strategic projects as automation reduced the manual workload.

Case Study 16: Tackling Shadow IT

Scenario: Employees bypassed IT policies by using unauthorized tools, creating security risks.

IT Manager's Role:

- **Policy Update:** Established a transparent approval process for software and tool usage.
- **Awareness Campaign:** Conducted seminars highlighting the risks of shadow IT.
- **Monitoring:** Deployed tools to detect unauthorized applications on the network.

Outcome: Security risks were minimized, and employees gained a better understanding of approved tools.

Case Study 17: Case Study: Creating a Diversity Hiring Program

Scenario: The IT team lacked diversity, limiting perspectives and problem-solving abilities.

IT Manager's Role:

- **Outreach Programs:** Partnered with universities and organizations to recruit diverse talent.
- **Inclusive Culture:** Fostered an inclusive onboarding process.
- **Metrics:** Ensured ongoing monitoring of diversity initiatives for continual improvement.

Outcome: The team became more collaborative and innovative, benefiting from a variety of perspectives.

Case Study 18: Case Study: Optimizing Remote Work Tools

Scenario: The sudden transition to remote work created inefficiencies in collaboration and security.

IT Manager's Role:

- **Tool Selection:** Evaluated and implemented secure remote collaboration tools.
- **Standardization:** Established consistent file-sharing protocols to avoid duplication.
- **Security:** Rolled out VPNs and multi-factor authentication.

Outcome: Team collaboration improved, and security protocols ensured safe remote operations.

Case Study 19: Vendor Lock-In Avoidance

Scenario: A company realized its over-reliance on a single cloud provider could lead to high costs and risks.

IT Manager's Role:

- **Strategy Development:** Designed a multi-cloud strategy with redundant workloads.

- **Negotiation:** Secured flexible terms with vendors through renegotiated contracts.

- **Team Training:** Upskilled staff on managing hybrid cloud environments.

Outcome: The organization achieved a more balanced and cost-effective cloud infrastructure.

Case Study 20: Introducing Employee Wellness Tech

Scenario: High stress levels in the IT team affected morale and productivity.

IT Manager's Role:

- **Technology Solutions:** Implemented wellness apps for meditation and stress management.

- **Flexible Schedules:** Created a flexible work policy during high-stress periods.

- **Feedback Mechanism:** Introduced anonymous surveys to monitor team well-being.

Outcome: The team felt more supported, leading to improved engagement and reduced burnout.

Appendix B: Glossary of Key IT Management Terms

1. **Access Control** Managing and restricting user access to data and systems based on roles or policies.

2. **Agile™ Methodology** A flexible approach to project management that promotes iterative development and collaboration.

3. **API (Application Programming Interface)** Protocols allowing different software systems to communicate.

4. **Asset Management** Tracking and optimizing the lifecycle of IT assets, including hardware and software.

5. **Availability** The percentage of time a system is operational and accessible.

6. **Backup and Recovery** Processes for duplicating data and restoring it in case of loss or corruption.

7. **Bandwidth** The amount of data transferable over a network in a given time.

8. **Benchmarking** Comparing performance metrics to industry standards or best practices.

9. **Bottleneck** A point in a system where performance is limited or delayed.

10. **BYOD (Bring Your Own Device)** A policy enabling employees to use personal devices for work.

11. **Capacity Planning** Ensuring IT resources can meet current and future demands.

12. **Change Management** Strategies to guide teams through organizational or technological changes.

13. **Cloud Computing** On-demand access to computing resources like servers, storage, and applications via the internet.

14. **Compliance** Adhering to laws, regulations, and standards.

15. **Continuous Integration (CI)** The practice of merging

code changes frequently to detect errors early.

16. Continuous Deployment (CD) Automating the release of software updates directly to production.

17. Cybersecurity Protecting systems and data from unauthorized access and attacks.

18. Data Governance Frameworks for managing data integrity, security, and usability.

19. Data Migration The process of moving data between storage systems or formats.

20. Disaster Recovery (DR) Plans and procedures for restoring IT systems after a catastrophic event.

21. Downtime The period when a system is unavailable or non-operational.

22. Endpoint Security Measures to protect devices that connect to a network, like laptops and mobile phones.

23. Encryption Encoding data to protect it from unauthorized access.

24. Enterprise Resource Planning (ERP) Software for managing business processes across departments.

25. Firewall A security device that filters traffic to and from a network.

26. High Availability (HA) Ensuring a system remains operational with minimal downtime.

27. Hybrid Cloud Combining private and public cloud solutions for flexible resource management.

28. Incident Management Addressing and resolving IT service disruptions.

29. Internet of Things (IoT) Interconnected devices that collect and exchange data.

30. ITIL (Information Technology Infrastructure Library) A framework for IT service management best practices.

31. KPI (Key Performance Indicator) Metrics to measure the success of IT initiatives.

32. Load Balancing Distributing network or application traffic across servers to optimize performance.

33. Managed Services Outsourcing IT operations to third-party providers.

34. Microservices An architectural style where applications are built as a suite of small, independent services.

35. Middleware Software that bridges different applications or systems.

36. Network Monitoring Tracking network performance and identifying issues.

37. On-Premises Deploying and running software or hardware within a company's physical location.

38. Patch Management Updating software to fix vulnerabilities and improve functionality.

39. Penetration Testing Simulating attacks to find and fix security vulnerabilities.

40. Phishing A cyberattack that tricks users into revealing sensitive information.

41. Privacy Impact Assessment (PIA) Evaluating how systems and processes affect data privacy.

42. Problem Management Identifying and resolving root causes of IT issues.

43. Project Management Office (PMO) A centralized team that standardizes project management practices.

44. Proxy Server An intermediary server that processes client requests.

45. Quality Assurance (QA) Ensuring that software meets specified quality standards.

46. Redundancy Adding duplicate systems or components for reliability.

47. Remote Monitoring and Management (RMM) Managing IT infrastructure remotely using specialized tools.

48. Resilience A system's ability to recover quickly from disruptions.

49. Risk Assessment Identifying and evaluating risks to IT systems and processes.

50. Role-Based Access Control (RBAC) Restricting access to systems based on user roles.

51. Root Cause Analysis (RCA) Investigating the primary causes of issues.

52. Scalability The ability of a system to grow and handle increased demand.

53. SD-WAN (Software-Defined Wide Area Network) A virtual WAN architecture for centralized network control.

54. Security Information and Event Management (SIEM) Tools for real-time analysis of security alerts.

55. Service Desk A single point of contact for IT support and services.

56. Service Level Agreement (SLA) A contract defining the expected service levels between a provider and customer.

57. Shadow IT Unapproved use of IT systems, applications, or devices.

58. Single Sign-On (SSO) Allowing users to log in to multiple systems with one set of credentials.

59. Smart Goals A framework for setting Specific, Measurable, Achievable, Relevant, and Time-bound objectives.

60. Stakeholder Anyone with an interest in a project or system.

61. Storage Area Network (SAN) A high-speed network that connects storage devices.

62. Threat Intelligence Data about potential cyber threats to improve security defenses.

63. Total Cost of Ownership (TCO) The full cost of owning and operating IT systems.

64. Troubleshooting Identifying and resolving IT issues.

65. Two-Factor Authentication (2FA) A security process requiring two forms of verification.

66. Uptime The percentage of time a system remains operational.

67. Version Control Tracking changes to files and coordinating work among teams.

68. Virtual Machine (VM) A software-based emulation of a physical computer.

69. Virtual Private Network (VPN) A secure connection over the internet.

70. Vulnerability Management Identifying, evaluating, and mitigating IT vulnerabilities.

71. Workflow Automation Using tools to automate repetitive IT tasks.

72. Zero Downtime Deployment Releasing updates without service interruptions.

73. Zero Trust Architecture A security model that assumes all users and devices are untrusted by default.

74. Access Management Processes for granting or restricting user permissions to systems and data.

75. Actionable Insight Data analysis results that can guide decision-making or prompt actions.

76. Adaptive Leadership A leadership style emphasizing flexibility to meet changing demands.

77. Alert Fatigue Desensitization to system alerts due to an overwhelming number of notifications.

78. Application Lifecycle Management (ALM) Managing the development, deployment, and maintenance of software applications.

79. Authentication The process of verifying a user's identity before granting access.

80. Business Continuity Plan (BCP) A strategy to ensure critical business operations can continue during disruptions.

81. Capacity Utilization The extent to which an organization's IT resources are being used effectively.

82. Centralized Logging Aggregating logs from multiple systems in a single location for easier monitoring.

83. Configuration Management Maintaining consistency in system settings and configurations.

84. Containerization Packaging software and dependencies into isolated units for portability.

85. Continuous Monitoring Ongoing surveillance of IT systems to detect issues or breaches.

86. Credential Management Storing and managing user credentials securely.

87. Critical Path Method (CPM) A project management tool for scheduling tasks to meet deadlines efficiently.

88. Customer Relationship Management (CRM) Software for managing interactions with current and potential customers.

89. Data Integrity Ensuring the accuracy and consistency of data over its lifecycle.

90. Data Retention Policy Guidelines for how long data should be stored and when it should be deleted.

91. Dependency Mapping Identifying relationships between IT components to manage changes effectively.

92. DevSecOps Integrating security practices into the DevOps process.

93. Digital Transformation The adoption of digital technologies to improve business processes.

94. Elasticity A system's ability to scale up or down based on demand dynamically.

95. End-of-Life (EOL) The point when a product or system is no longer supported by the vendor.

96. Governance, Risk, and Compliance (GRC) A framework for managing organizational governance, risk, and compliance.

97. Green IT Practices to reduce the environmental impact of IT operations.

98. Incident Response Plan (IRP) A predefined approach for responding to IT incidents.

99. Information Architecture (IA) The organization of data and systems to optimize usability and performance.

100. IT Asset Disposal (ITAD) Securely decommissioning and recycling obsolete IT equipment.

TRADEMARKS AND ACKNOWLEDGMENTS

The trademarks and registered trademarks mentioned in this book are the property of their respective owners. Below is a list of trademarks cited and their owners:

- **Microsoft®, Microsoft Azure®, Azure™, Azure Storage™, Azure Active Directory™, Azure Key Vault™, Azure DevOps®, Microsoft SharePoint®, Microsoft Project®, Power BI®, Microsoft Azure Solutions™, Teams™** – Microsoft Corporation
- **AWS™, AWS Solutions Architect®, AWS WorkDocs®** – Amazon Web Services, Inc.
- **Google®, Google Drive®, Google Jamboard®** – Google LLC
- **GitHub®** – GitHub, Inc.
- **Jira®, Trello®, Monday.com®** – Atlassian Corporation Plc and Monday.com Ltd. respectively
- **Docker®** – Docker, Inc.
- **Nagios™** – Nagios Enterprises, LLC
- **Minitab®** – Minitab, LLC
- **Myers-Briggs®, ISTJ in MBTI®, ENTJ in MBTI®** – The Myers & Briggs Foundation

- **DISC®** – Inscape Publishing, Inc.
- **CISSP®** – International Information System Security Certification Consortium (ISC)²
- **CEH®** – EC-Council
- **CompTIA Security+®** – CompTIA, Inc.
- **Jenkins™** – Jenkins project
- **Slack®** – Slack Technologies, LLC
- **Zabbix®** – Zabbix LLC
- **CrowdStrike®, CrowdStrike Falcon®** – CrowdStrike, Inc.
- **Snort®, ClamAV®** – Cisco Systems, Inc.
- **SigmaXL®** – SigmaXL, Inc.
- **Six Sigma®** – Motorola, Inc.
- **Scrum™, Certified Scrum Master®** – Scrum Alliance, Inc.
- **Coursera®** – Coursera, Inc.
- **LinkedIn Learning®** – LinkedIn Corporation
- **ITIL® Foundation** – AXELOS Limited
- **PMP®** – Project Management Institute (PMI)
- **Veeam®** – Veeam Software
- **Tableau®** – Tableau Software, LLC
- **Apptio®** – Apptio, Inc.
- **ServiceNow®** – ServiceNow, Inc.
- **Wazuh®** – Wazuh, Inc.
- **LibreNMS™** – LibreNMS project
- **PRTG Network Monitor®** – Paessler AG
- **Datadog®** – Datadog, Inc.
- **SentinelOne®** – SentinelOne, Inc.

- **Splunk®** – Splunk Inc.
- **McKinsey®** – McKinsey & Company
- **BetterUp®** – BetterUp, Inc.
- **Humantelligence®** – Humantelligence, Inc.
- **Pluralsight®** – Pluralsight, Inc.

These trademarks are acknowledged with respect for their intellectual property rights and contributions to the fields they serve.

www.ingramcontent.com/pod-product-compliance
Lightning Source LLC
Chambersburg PA
CBHW040856210326
41597CB00029B/4869